M000163940

Sleepy Eye
Dreams

Barbara Deines

jujapa
hansville

press
washington

ISBN-13: 978-1-952493-22-5

Author : Barbara Deines
Cover: Kozakura from Fiverr.com
Illustrator: Michele Kapusta from Fiverr.com

Published:
Jujapa Press, LLC
PO Box 269
Hansville, Wa 98340

NOTE: The views, preferences and opinions expressed by the authors in these pages belong solely to the author and do not necessarily reflect the views, preferences and opinions of Jujapa Press, LLC, or anyone other than the author.

Dedication

Dedicated to my children and children-in-law, Sarah, Ben, Colin and Whitney, to my grand-children, Peter, Jacob and Samara, to my nephew, Nigel and to my niece, Tracy. They were all young once.

Acknowledgements

The title *Sleepy Eye Dreams* comes from the name of a small town in south central Minnesota just northwest of the Cottonwood River. It is named for Chief Sleepy Eye or Ishtakhaba of the Sisseton Wahpeton Oyate.

The first acknowledgement therefore is of the land of the Sisseton Wahpeton Oyate. The mistreatment of the people of that land has cast a long shadow in the history of that region and of the United States. My father grew up in Sleepy Eye and he is the inspiration for the boy Phil who narrates my story. His name was also Phil and in many ways he was just like the boy in the story. He loved reading, sports and above all his family. He was an authentic individual who was always true to himself.

I have been writing nearly all my life and I am grateful for the encouragement I have received along the way. I especially want to recognize the late American historian and professor at Colorado State University, Charles Bayard. Dr. Bayard offered lengthy criticisms and terse affirmations. He wrote on one of my papers "You can write." Those three short words have boosted my spirits for all the decades that have followed.

I want to thank those readers who made suggestions and much improved the narrative - John Henley, Cassie Winter and my former student Emma Van Dyke.

Thanks also to Michele Kapusta for the wonderful chapter line drawings and to Kozakura of Fiverr for her remarkable cover illustration.

The book would not have gone to print at all without the help of Clark Parsons who has been so patient with my greenhornedness. He steered the whole process with expertise and skill.

Most of all I want to thank my family who cheered me on - especially my husband Stephen who read every single word - multiple times - and who laughed and cried with me as the story unfolded.

Foreword

The following is a work of fiction. It comes largely from a world I have visited in my own imagination. But that world has been shaped and informed by the stories I have heard, told mostly by my father. It is as true a place as I can make it.

Contents

Chapter One: Chicken Swoon

It was the hottest day of that summer so far. There was not a single cloud in the sky and everything was dry and dusty. We still lived on the farm then - just north of town - my pa, ma, two sisters, three brothers and me. I was the oldest boy so Pa and Ma depended on me for things my little brothers weren't old enough to do. Farms are a lot of work. Every day there are chores that have to be done. At least my parents seemed to think so.

Ma had sent me to put the chickens in the hutch over an hour before. She was afraid that it was too hot out in their yard and that they needed to be out of glaring sun. On my way to put the chickens in I took a short detour to the creek bottom which was shaded by cottonwood trees along both sides of its banks. It was a lot cooler down there than up at the chicken yard. As long as I was right there I thought I might toss some stones in the water to see if I could make them skip. I tried a long, flat one that looked like it had good potential. No luck. Pa could skip one every time and I had watched him to see if I could get the hang of it. So far I hadn't been able to get any to hop along the surface like his did. I kept trying and one or two slid in sideways instead of falling right to the bottom so I figured I was making progress. Since I was right there by the water I naturally thought it was worth wading in a ways - just to cool my feet. The creek made a turn at that point which created a little eddy and a small pool. The deepest part was probably only two feet this time of year. Little by little I made all the way out to the middle. Maybe wading was not quite the right word. By the time I got back up on the bank my overalls were soaked and even my hair was wet. Boy did that feel good. Not nearly as good as swimming in the lake though.

I was hoping Pa might take us to the lake when he got home from work. It was sure hot enough. He did sometimes have all the kids, except my baby brother, pile into the truck and then head out to Sleepy Eye Lake. That was the lake just east of our farm. It was a good lake - both for swimming and fishing. Spring fed, it stayed cool enough for swimming even into the dog days of August. It had plenty of fish too - crappies, walleye, and sunfish. They were all good to eat but I liked crappies best. Ma fried them up until they were white and flaky.

Pa had taken me fishing just the Saturday before. It had not been such a hot day and we were out on the lake early. Sitting in the soft morning light I was almost cold. The lake was still - not even a light breeze - and we could hear the cry of the loon somewhere beyond us. Finally we spotted him - Pa thought it was a male - making his rounds by the shore. He swam along looking all majestic and regal. Have you ever heard the call of the loon? It's eerie but in a good way. I liked to hear it best when I was with Pa. He told me a Sioux story about Loon who went all the way down to the deepest part of the water and brought back mud. The mud was used to create World. That happened a long time ago. The story made sense because if you have ever watched loons you know they disappear for a long time when they go under the water. Pa and I sat in the boat and kept an eye on the one that was floating near us. As soon as he went down, we each picked a spot on the surface where we thought he would reappear.

Then we waited…and waited…and waited. Every time we almost gave up - decided he'd gone to another part of the lake - then up he'd pop. Neither of us had picked exactly the right spot but we each got close a couple of times. Finally, he went down and never came up again where we could see him. Pa thought we should row over to another part of the lake where he had seen a fish jump. He let me squeeze in next to him so I could row on one side. We were slow but we weren't in a hurry. When the two of us were out on the lake together we were the only people in the world and there didn't seem to be any time before or any time after.

Pa caught two bass that morning. The first one we called Daddy Bass and the next we called Bass, Jr. Pa thought the big one weighed about seven or eight pounds but he looked bigger than that to me. He had fought hard too - like a fish who's been around. I caught one nice little sunny. Pa said we would have Ma fry them up for breakfast.

I could think about that cool lake all I wanted but I still had those chickens to deal with on a hot day. Dripping wet from my wade, I left my creek bottom pursuits and headed toward the chicken coop. On my way I had to pass the barn. Ours was not a big red barn like those of many of our neighbors. We had more of an oversized shed that we used like a barn. It had a loft though and right now I could see in the darkness of the interior a noose hanging from one of the boards in the loft floor. I could see it plain as day. Maybe not quite. It was so bright where I was and dark as night in the barn. It was almost totally black except that the shed floor and walls had little pale streaks of light where the sunshine seeped through the boards. The shards of light made the noose stand out and I could see that it was swaying. Hardly any movement in the air at all but it was swaying - just a little. I stood and stared at it because I couldn't think what to do. I had to find somebody - by somebody I meant one of my sisters or brothers.

My oldest sister Mabel was out by the cistern tending to some brand new kittens. She had them in a box and was stuffing rags all around. The mother cat must have been hunting mice because she was nowhere to be seen. Getting Mabel away from those kittens was not going to be easy.

"There's a ghost in the barn," I started right out with my best shot.

"I doubt that." Mabel was the practical type.

"I saw a sure ghost-sign just now. There's a noose hanging from the loft and it's swaying. Nothing to make it sway but it is." I was pretty proud of the soundness of my evidence. It got her interested at any rate.

"No," she said standing at the barn door, "that is not a true ghost-sign for two reasons. For one thing it's not even a noose. It just looks like one. A noose has coiled-up-part for cinching around the neck tight," she demonstrated with her hands on my neck until I told her to cut it out. "This one," she pointed at my noose, "is just twisted and would come right apart when you tried to hang somebody. Second," she said with an impatient sigh, "it's only bailing wire," with that she turned and left and went back to her kittens. Of course, we both knew it was a noose. How it got there was hard to say but I guessed it was something that could be seen but not touched. I planned to stay away from the barn for as long as I could. I might even get one of my sisters or brothers to go with me next time I had to go in there.

My hair and clothes were almost dry and I felt hot and sticky all over again - also the chickens were making a terrific racket. Oh good grief, the chickens! I raced as fast as I could to the chicken yard. There was not a spot of shade and the chickens were squawking like crazy in the heat. That is all but one was squawking like crazy. The one that wasn't was lying stock-still in the middle of the yard in a feathery heap. Boy, now I was going to get it for sure. Ma had been right. The heat had killed that poor chicken. And it was my fault. If only I had gone right away when Ma said that chicken would still be alive. I was in big trouble. I wouldn't just get it from Ma either; Pa would probably get worked up about it too. My pa was a mild man and generally easy-going but he did have a line that could be crossed. A dead chicken seemed likely to be on the other side of that line.

There was really only one thing I could do. I got behind the mass of squawking chickens and herded them into the hutch. They were surprisingly timid considering the awful racket they were making and I got them in without too much trouble. The hutch was close and dusty but it was out of the blazing sun and the chickens were quick to calm down once they were inside and out of the glare. Even the rooster, Mr. Combs, Pa called him as a joke on our red-headed neighbor Mr. Holmes, went in without a fuss and grew quiet in the near-darkness of the hutch. Normally that Mr. Combs would have been on the warpath as soon as he saw anybody in the yard. He usually waited until an intruder had his or her back turned and then he attacked with talons out ready to dig into tender flesh. The only way I had found to avoid the wrath of Mr. Combs was to walk backwards. It wasn't easy to walk backwards while feeding chickens and collecting eggs but it could be done. I had become an expert at it myself. Today though Mr. Combs had been overcome by the heat just like the rest and didn't seem to have the energy for an attack.

Once I had the chickens in the hutch, I thought to give them fresh water which meant going up to the pump. I didn't really want to go up that way because Ma might spot me but, unless I wanted another dead chicken on my hands, I knew

I'd better try. I decided I would approach the pump from around behind the hutch and the vegetable garden-that way I could disappear into the bushes if I saw Ma coming. I made it to the pump all right but then I spotted her walking out of the back door - probably headed to the garden. I heard her call my name, "Phil," in a not-angry way so I knew I was not in trouble yet. She was carrying my baby brother Vernon. Vernon had a pink face with chubby cheeks. One of our aunts thought he looked like a baby rabbit, because he was so adorable, so most everyone called him Bunny. I did not think my brother looked like a bunny because his ears were normal human ears so I had decided not to call him Bunny but I usually forgot that I decided that and called him Bunny anyway. Pa never called him Bunny because he was named after his own brother whose name was Vernon, of course, and so he liked to call him that. Uncle Vernon lived in Ohio and I had not met him at that time.

I thought I could get away with not answering Ma for now because she would probably think I just didn't hear her. I ran back to the hutch with a bucket of cool water as quietly as I could through the bushes. I picked up the chicken's watering can and emptied out the stale water which had lots of tiny feathers and bits of feed floating in it. Then I refilled the can with the pump water. The chickens were sure happy with that fresh water – especially Mr. Combs who bumped everyone else out of the way to get in first. I would have liked to stay and watch the chickens squabble over turns at the water but I still had work to do. I slipped out the door and latched it. There was that poor, dead chicken still in a heap in the middle of the yard. I picked it up by its scaly feet and carried it out, head hanging and flopping. I heard Ma call again – still not angry but a little louder and slower so I knew I had better answer soon. My plan had been to bury the dead hen and be done with it but with Ma yelling for me, I didn't figure I had time for that. Instead I took it way behind the house on the creek side and put it down under a small stand of trees. I did my best to cover it with dried leaves and bits of moss. It seemed to me that no matter how much I piled on it, its white feathers always showed through. I worked at it as long as I dared and then sauntered kind of slow and casual back toward the house. I didn't want to look suspicious.

"Philip Stanley!" Now Ma's call was loud and sharp and included my middle name. I walked a little faster when I came in sight of her so she could see I was responding.

"What are you up to?" Ma wanted to know. "Why don't you answer when I call you?"

"I couldn't hear you," I said without thinking.

"If you didn't hear me, how did you know I called?" was her logical response. I paused in order to think of something to offer in return but she was not interested.

"Did you take care of them chickens like I told you to?"

"Yup."

"Did you think to get the eggs?"

"Oh, I forgot the eggs." I added before she could say anything more: "I'll go get 'em right now." I turned to leave when she caught me by the strap of my overalls.

"Aren't you forgetting something?"

Dead chickens don't lay eggs? No, what she really said was, "You need the basket to put 'em in."

I ran as fast as I could to the back porch, grabbed the basket and ran past her and Bunny toward the chicken yard.

"Look good under the hay. Don't forget," she called after me.

It was still stuffy and full of flying dust in the hutch. But I gathered eggs methodically. I figured the more eggs the better. I thought maybe if I did all the feeding and watering of the chickens and gathered all the eggs, they might never find out. Not even Ma was going to suddenly take it to her head to go out and count chickens. And, after all, they all looked pretty much alike - some larger, some smaller. All hens except for Mr. Combs. Unless you lined 'em up it would take a long time to determine there was one less chicken in the yard.

Not that I felt all that easy about my prospects. The chickens were no small matter at our place. With eight mouths to feed, Ma depended on the daily supply of eggs. Pa worked hard and took good care of all of us but buying eggs was costly and an unplanned-for expense. Every single chicken counted to our family.

I found ten eggs but the close, stuffy space made me feel light-headed and a little sick to my stomach. I carried the full basket up toward the house but Ma was no longer standing there. I went inside and set the basket on the kitchen table. There didn't seem to be anybody else inside the house. The curtains were all drawn against the strong, summer sun and there was not a sound. I didn't know where Ma and Bunny had gone. Pa was still out on his rounds picking up cream from local dairy farmers. My sister Maude was helping our aunt put up her beets. In the morning, Ma had sent her over there because her sister Ellie had no daughters of her own. Maude liked the chance to spend the day in town and Ellie was a cheerful woman who liked to spoil her some when she had the chance. Mabel was probably still tending those kittens and I couldn't think where the other two boys might be. The last time I saw them they had been carting water from the pigs' trough, where they could reach it through the fence, over to the shade behind the corn crib. There they were busy making mud cakes and drying them on nearby rocks. But that was probably more than an hour ago. I didn't suppose they could still be at it.

Slanted light fell across the kitchen through the muslin curtains. The wobbling rays gave me a whirling sensation and I felt like I had to lie down. I wandered around the house looking for a place. I didn't suppose I was allowed to mess up the bed in the middle of the day unless I had a fever and I knew the parlor was off-limits. I opened the front door to the shaded side of the house. There was the glider. Perfect. The wood slates had not absorbed the day's heat and the spaces between them let the air move around my sweaty body. I lay down. With the glider swaying gently under me, I fell asleep. In my dream, I could hear people calling my name from way far away. I tried to go to them but the door kept moving farther away when I tried to reach out for the knob. I reached and reached but the door was never any closer. Then the glider creaked and I woke up. Things were very confused. The dream voices now seemed more like real ones. I thought they might be getting closer but they were still a jumble. I had to struggle to stay awake and try to make out what they were saying. Someone really was saying my name. Pa maybe but maybe Ma too. No one seemed to know where I was. Bunny was crying or he might have been laughing. I heard my sister Mabel's voice but I couldn't quite make out what she said.

Chicken. That was it. She had said something about a chicken. Oh brother. My goose was cooked. Chicken anyway.

Had my brothers found the stashed bird? My parents would never understand. First I killed it and then I hid it.

I formulated a plan as quickly as I could. First, I would tip-toe off the porch in the direction of the oak trees along the road. Then I would make a dash as fast as I could across the road and hide in the Bekke's barn. As soon as it was dark, I would slip back in the house and pack up my shoes, a sweater, some bread, some gooseberry pie -which I had seen this morning sitting on the kitchen counter - and whatever other food I could carry. I would walk all the way to the highway and there, when it was light, I would hitch a ride to the Cities. They wouldn't know I was really gone until morning and then they'd be sorry. Ma would probably cry. I tried to imagine Ma crying but since I had never seen her cry, it was hard. Pa might even cry. At least he would put his head down and groan like when he had to shoot that old lame horse named Woody. It was a good plan and I was just getting ready to put into action when the screen door opened and Pa put his head out.

"Philip, what are you up to?"

Running away from home? No, not a good answer. "I was takin' a nap."

"Well, you better get up now and come around back. Apparently there's some trouble about a chicken."

I had no choice but to go. I followed Pa with a sinking heart. I was not sure what the punishment for killing a chicken might be. It had to be something worthy of the deed - that much I was sure of. In our family Ma was usually in charge of discipline. That was because she was around mostly and because she thought we "needed to learn a lesson." Up to that point I had primarily learned my lessons by sitting in a corner of the parlor. There was even a chair for it. It was an ancient, wooden chair with a cane seat made especially for a child. It had been passed down for generations, Ma said. When I had to sit in that old chair I tried to imagine some pioneer boy sitting there just like me. I often wondered what his crime had been. I sometimes spent my whole time in the corner thinking up bad things that pioneer boy had done and completely forgetting to learn my lesson. Having Pa take over had to raise the stakes beyond sitting in the corner. I figured that much. Even though he was a mild-mannered man a dead chicken which had been secretly buried was probably even more than he could tolerate.

As I ran to catch up with Pa - he seemed to be in an awful hurry - I wasn't just thinking of my punishment. I was wishing I could go back a couple of hours and take care of the chickens as soon as Ma told me to. I felt like I had let her and Pa down. How could I make it up to them? Maybe I could stop eating eggs? Or at least only have one for breakfast instead of two. If only I could go back in time …. and then there was the dead chicken. Only it wasn't dead any more. It was up and running around in the yard. And it wasn't any other chicken. I could tell it was the same chicken because here and there it had moss and leaves still stuck on its white feathers.

I stood there gaping until I heard Pa say, "You get behind her and walk toward the yard. I am going to open the gate and then we can get on either side of her and shoo her in. She'll want to get in there where the feed and water are." He grinned, "She just might not know she wants to go in."

I didn't have much time to consider how that dead chicken had come back to life. I just did what Pa told me. I had to zigzag back and forth with my arms spread wide because I didn't make a very big obstacle by myself. By the time I got even with Pa, the chicken was running in circles and squawking up a storm - as if she had never been dead. Finally, when we both walked toward her at once she bee-lined it for the yard. Pa closed the gate and laughed, "I guess she decided she did want to go in."

He turned to me and said, "Good work. That was one excited bird. I could never have gotten her in by myself." He tousled my mop of sun-bleached hair.

"Time to eat!" Pa said and the two of us headed back to the house.

Just before we went in - we could already smell supper through the screen door - Pa turned to me and asked, "So how did that chicken get out of the yard anyway?"

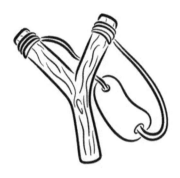

Chapter Two: Shadows

Ma always said I either had my head in the clouds or in a book. I don't know about the clouds but I did like to read. The only actual book we had in our house was the Bible. It sat all solemn on a small table in the front room. I can't remember anyone reading it. In the front it had a list of my grandparents and their parents. I liked to open it sometimes and look at the fancy writing.

My teacher Miss Jordahl let me borrow books sometimes though. Lately I had been reading a book about a hollow tree that was pretty good. Sometimes when I was reading a story like that I liked to add parts of my own. In the one about the hollow tree there was a crow, a raccoon, and a possum in the deep woods so I thought what if there was also a bobcat or a bear or a wolf in the woods? That would sure add some excitement to the plot.

At school we learned to read from books called *Readers*. They were all right but I got tired of the plain-old stories. I went through them so fast Miss Jordahl thought I was being lazy.

One day she said to me, "Philip, why is your *Reader* closed on your desk?"

"I'm finished."

"Do you mean you do not want to read it any more? Is it too difficult?"

"I mean I read it. I finished the reading." I was sorry for the snickers that followed. Miss Jordahl had a big job. There were about forty of us in the school and some did not like being there so much. The Munson twins were the oldest. They were almost a foot taller than Miss Jordahl and they thought it was funny to give her a hard time. Spit wads were their specialty which didn't take much imagination but never failed to entertain them.

"Now Ronald, suppose you pick those bits of paper up off the floor. Robert, you may help. Both of you may see me after school."

Miss Jordahl didn't raise her voice or anything but I could tell she was just about to cry. An adult can get pretty tired of spit wads I guess. The twins didn't argue. They weren't really so bad. They were just ready to be done with school. After they finished eighth grade, they both went to work on farms. When school was over that day, I noticed Ron out back by the shed filling the coal scuttle without Miss Jordahl even asking him.

Besides reading, we had arithmetic, penmanship, geography and history. We memorized all forty-eight states and their capitals. I decided one day I would go to every state there was. I supposed that would take me at least a month – to get to all of them. I wanted especially to go to Ohio where my pa was from.

Miss Jordahl showed us on a big map where each state was and where the capital was. She used a long wooden pointer. I wondered if she ever thought she might like to whack one of the Munson twins with that pointer. I wouldn't blame her.

Some of the states were much bigger than ours and some a lot smaller but Minnesota was the most northern state in the whole country. I felt quite proud of our northern-ness.

The day the twins threw the spit wads, Miss Jordahl taught us about the Dakota War of 1862. That took place right near where we lived so everyone was pretty interested. The town we were closest to was named after a Dakota chief named Sleepy Eye. He had a real name which was Ishtabkhaba but I don't think Miss Jordahl knew that because she didn't mention it. I guess he looked sleepy to somebody but in the pictures they didn't show that. My oldest sister Mabel told me the true name of Sleepy Eye. Sometimes she knew things the teacher didn't.

All the way home that day I thought about the Dakota War. Having a war happen right where you live seemed to me a strange thing. Wars, in my experience, had been far away. Like the one in Europe. I couldn't quite figure out what the war around here had been about. If everybody had been so mad at the Dakotas why did they name the whole town after a chief? That didn't make much sense. Also where were they? The Dakotas? Nobody in my school. None of my neighbors. I asked Mabel later that night and she told me that they left.

"What do you mean they left? Where'd they go?"

"They went to live on reservations," Mabel said.

"What's a reservation?"

"A place where Indians live. Stop asking so many questions."

Usually people say to stop asking so many questions when they don't know the answer. I figured I would ask Miss Jordahl the next day but she had moved on to Father Hennepin and the voyageurs so I never got a chance.

The next Saturday my parents went to New Ulm. That was the county seat and it was a big town. I normally would have wanted to go along but the day before, my sister Maude for no particular reason had taken a log bridge over a dry creek bed on the way home from school. Everyone else had just walked right through the creek bed. It was too bad for Maudie because hornets had built their nest in that log and they went after her with a fury. She ran and screamed but that didn't do much good. In the end, she was covered all over with hot, red welts. Ma had done everything she could do to ease the pain including an old Sioux cure that involved smashing goldenrod flowers into a paste. I stood over her while she ground up the yellow petals and asked what was she doing, why did it work, would it hurt when she rubbed it on, and why did it smell like that until she told me to go fill the wood bin which was odd because I had filled it only an hour before. The paste did seem to help some though, at least when it first went on, but there were just too many bites.

The ride into New Ulm sounded like torture to Maudie so Mabel, the oldest, had offered to stay home with her and I had begged to stay as well. The allures of New Ulm seemed distant while the warm, late autumn morning was right there at hand. Pa had not thought long; three at home was better than two especially when one was laid-up. The decision was made – they had to get on the road – so neither Pa nor Ma had time to think up extra chores for me to do as long as I was staying. Miraculous. As soon as my parents had pulled out, I rushed to do what I knew had to be done that day. Pump the water, stack cookstove wood in the kitchen, feed the chickens, geese, and pigs. Pa had already taken care of our one milk cow and Ma had watered her flower pots before they left. It had rained earlier in the week so the fall vegetables would not need watering for a day or two. I was totally and completely free. As I grabbed my slingshot I called out to Mabel, "I'm goin' to hunt birds."

Mabel was four years older and motherly by nature. She called back something about my needing to be in hearing distance – this was a rule our ma had – but I was only half-listening to her and decided as long as I was back before the next meal I would be okay.

The sky was achingly blue with big fair-weather clouds that might look like giants or dragons if I had had time to study them. I stuck my slingshot in the back pocket of my overalls and walked off in the direction of the creek. The same creek bed that I had waded into in mid-summer was now almost completely dry. It made a passable trail and I could walk a good way on it before I found open country.

I had wandered pretty far away from 'hearing distance' when I realized that I didn't know exactly where I was. I had left the creek bed some time before and found myself in a stand of trees. I could tell the trees were oaks by the windy shape of the leaves. The realization that I might be lost gave me a nice spooky feeling. I was not really afraid though. I had my slingshot. The oaks around me were just starting to change color. Some leaves were mostly still green with gold edges, some were all gold, some were bright orange and just a few were all brown. It had been such a dry fall that some leaves had already fallen on the ground and they crunched when I walked. There were acorns on the ground too. Their pointed ends really hurt my bare feet. Even though there was hardly any breeze I could still hear the leaves on the trees rustle when the air caught them. They are big trees – oaks. In a story Miss Jordahl told us the Greek god Zeus turned somebody into an oak tree. It was a reward – becoming an oak tree – for being a good host. I think I would want a different reward myself. Remembering the story made me feel like I was being watched. The tree people stood their ground all around me. Was it their murmurs I could hear?

On the opposite edge of the oak stand, I thought I saw a shadow glide along between two trees. It could have been a deer – too big for my slingshot – but probably something smaller. Pa and my uncle had spotted a bobcat once where the woods opened onto an alfalfa field and I thought a bobcat would be a very fine thing to see though I would have felt more like seeing it if Pa was there.

I decided I would slip behind one of the bigger trees and get a better look. I waited as long as I could stand it and then I slowly leaned out around the tree to see if I could spot what had made the shadow. Except for the rustling of the oak leaves, I had not heard a single sound since I had hidden behind the tree. I slid out, looked straight ahead and almost wet my pants. No more than two feet in front of me was another boy.

This other boy was in nearly every way a counterpart of myself – a little like looking in a mirror. He was the same height. He wore overalls and was barefoot and he held a slingshot in his right hand. Maybe he thought he'd seen a shadow too and was about to take aim. There was one difference between me and the other boy. This boy had coppery colored skin while mine was light. Even tanned by the summer, mine seemed pale next to his. My hair was still almost white from the long months of hot sun. The boy in front of me had shiny, black hair.

Without meaning to, I let out a gasp. The other boy laughed. I supposed it was funny so I laughed too.

"Hi. My name is Phil McCoy. What's yours?" I figured
we ought to introduce ourselves.

"Raymond," the boy said. He didn't say whether
Raymond was his first name or his last but he held his finger
up to his lips and motioned for me to follow him. He went
back in the direction he had come from – toward an opening
beyond the woods. He turned around once and said softly,
"Shh..." I was not sure if he meant to remind me or if he
thought I was making too much noise. I tried my best to take
light steps but the dry leaves still crackled under my feet. We
walked that way for about thirty yards or so to an old split rail
fence. Just on the other side of the fence was a derelict corn
field long since harvested and now abandoned. I had no idea
who it belonged to. Raymond pointed to the other side of the
field where there was another stand of trees. Here there were
oaks mixed with tall, slender cottonwoods.

"What?" I whispered to Raymond.

"Just at the corner of the fence line. Look up high," he
whispered back and grinned.

I looked toward the corner and saw one of the
cottonwoods bending way over. The top of the tree was
bobbing from the weight of a black form I finally spotted. I
could see that the dark shape was stretching itself out
between that cottonwood and the oak next to it. Then the
shape pulled back and made itself into a...bear. I had never

seen a bear before in my whole life. As far as I knew no one in my family had seen one. At least no one had ever talked about it. The bear was pretty far away from us – all the way across the field but it still seemed big. A ferocious-little-boy-eating-big bear.

"What should we do?" I whispered to Raymond. I was really hoping Raymond would be the one to suggest getting out of there so I wouldn't have to.

"Let's get really quiet and watch."

So we did. We found a spot sort of semi-hidden by wild blueberries and stood as still as we could.

I would have thought that big, old bear was about as high as it could go but while we watched it just kept climbing higher and higher and the cottonwood it was on kept bending further and further. I couldn't believe it didn't snap in two.

"Look! She's shaking that branch of the oak tree," Raymond gave my arm a soft punch so I didn't miss it.

Sure enough that's what it was doing – reaching out and giving it a good shake. The oak tree trembled as leaves and acorns showered down to the ground below.

"How do you know it's a she?" I had been wondering.

"Look below – under the tree – see?" He gestured toward the darkness below the oak. I could hardly see because of the shadows but there did seem to be something moving around on the ground. It was round and brown and came to a point on either end and then suddenly it split into two. Two more bears – both round and brown with one pointed end each. They must have been her cubs. Not little babies though. They weren't as big as their ma but they were still plenty big. And they were busy. They scooted all around under the oak while their ma shook the branch. It took me a minute to put it together but then it dawned on me. She was giving them their dinner – acorns – and they were scarfing them up as happy as could be. Just like my ma, the mama bear was taking care of her children. It was like watching a story book with pictures that had come to life. Raymond and I kept our lookout for a good long time. We didn't talk or even whisper, we just watched. The mama bear kept shaking that tree and the two cubs kept feasting below.

After a while though, we forgot about the being quiet part and when one of the cubs cuffed the other one, I supposed for getting in the way of its pile of acorns – we both laughed right out loud. Mama Bear instantly let go of the oak branch and straightened herself all the way up like she needed to see what was going on. The cubs kept munching along but she was still and alert. She was even bigger upright than she had been sideways and it seemed to me she was looking our way. Then she started down – not in a hurried way but she wasn't taking her time either. I guess she figured she'd better find out what all the noise was about. When she hit the ground, Raymond and I turned to face each other. Without saying a single word we agreed it was time to get out of there and we had better go fast. We slipped as silently as we could out from among the blueberries and crept back toward the stand of oaks. Boy those leaves were noisier than ever. I was afraid to look back until we got all the way to the other side of the woods. When I finally did, I thought sure Mama Bear would be coming up behind but she wasn't there. The cornfield and other woods were no longer in sight. I couldn't even see the split rail fence any more. It all just disappeared behind us.

When we got to the same path I had come on, we broke into a run – only in the other direction. It wasn't any kept path – just something made by animals – probably deer – but it seemed to go on forever. We ran until we were so out of breath we couldn't run anymore. We sat down on a couple of big rocks hoping we had put enough space between us and the big old bear.

Raymond in one long exhale, "That was close!"

"It sure was." Close didn't even seem to quite cover it. Each of us took out our slingshots as if to demonstrate we had been prepared all along. After a better look at Raymond's I was slow to show him mine. His slingshot was as smooth as glass and just as shiny. I ran my hand over it. There was not a rough place anywhere. His was bigger than mine too. I was surprised he could get his hand around it – the handle was so thick. Pa had helped me make mine. We had gone together into the woods near our house and found an ash because Pa said that was the best kind of wood for a slingshot. The right tree had to have a good, strong fork with both sides of the fork about the same size. Pa had made the holes for the rubber straps to thread through but then he had me do the sanding myself. Now I wished I had spent a little more time on my part.

Raymond didn't make any comment about the obvious difference, instead he with a grin, "Wanna do some huntin'?"

"Sure!"

So we left our rock easy-chairs and headed back into the woods. We walked a long way but we didn't have much luck. The crunching of the leaves made so much noise any animal small enough for us to take with our slingshots was long gone before we even saw it. We did scare up a grouse at one point but she flew high into the branches above us. We could see her up there fluffing her feathers, unthreatened by two small hunters below.

When we came to an old fence post we decided to shoot at pine cones instead. Since there were no pine trees right there we had to search around until we found even one but when we did there was a treasure trove of cones underneath it. We filled our arms with as many as we could carry and headed back to the fence post. Pine cones are extremely scratchy to carry. You should try it if you don't believe me.

We balanced the first cone on top of the fence post and held it in place with two small rocks. We decided on twenty paces to shoot from. That seemed fair since our feet were just about the same size. Raymond picked up a pebble and behind his back put it in one of his fists. Then he put both fists in front of him and I pointed to the one on the left. The pebble was there so I went first. I held the slingshot in my left hand and then with my right I drew back the leather pocket that held a good-sized rock. I squeezed my left eye closed, got my sites on the pine cone and let the ammunition fly. I was pretty close. My rock whizzed past the cone just to its left. Next time I needed to aim a little to the right. I thought maybe I'd claim it as a practice shot but Raymond stepped up so fast I never got the chance.

He followed the same steps as me only he took much longer. He could really hold the straps back for a long time. He pulled them even further back and then let go. His rock hit the fence post so hard the jolt knocked the pine cone on the ground. That made us howl.

After we recovered, we set the cone back up. I took aim again and moved my slingshot just a tiny bit to the right. Bingo. We had to use another cone. We figured out that if we hit our target we destroyed it. Raymond did not pull the rubber straps back quite so far on his second turn and hit the cone cleanly. I managed to hit a half dozen in all but Raymond hit almost twice that. He was stronger than he looked and I gave him a big slap on the back to show how much I admired his skill. He whirled around and I thought for a second he was going to punch me.

"You're a good shot," I said – by way of explanation.

He took in a deep breath and said – without a smile, "Yeah, you too." I think he meant it but I was still sorry I had slapped him.

My arms were tired from holding up the slingshot and I was feeling really hungry all of a sudden. I remembered that I had missed that next meal I had planned to be home for. As if he had read my mind, Raymond reached into one of his overall pockets and pulled out a small cloth. He unfolded the cloth and inside was a long, pink chunk of dried meat. He pulled it apart and handed a strip to me. It was so salty and delicious. We both had to chew and chew that leathery meat. Watching each other chew and chew made us laugh again and we crumpled to the ground laughing and chewing. We lay back and for a while watching clouds overhead drift along.

"A giraffe?" I offered but not with much conviction. Raymond only grunted. He was right, not much of a giraffe.

There was no more talk – just the sky, the warmth of the ground, and the small sounds of the world around us.

Then I sat up, "I think I better go." The sun was behind us now and moving well below the tops of the trees. Raymond sat up but didn't reply.

"Thanks for the meat….and everything." I thought shaking hands again was too formal so I gave him a light punch in the arm. He grinned and punched me just as lightly back. I guess he wasn't mad about the slap on the back anymore.

"Which way are you headed?" I asked him.

"That way." He pointed north. That wasn't the direction I needed to go so I gave him a wave and turned around. I didn't look back. I don't know if he did.

I walked along – not too fast, hoping to find the rocks we had sat down on earlier. I thought if I could get to them I might be able to retrace my steps back home. I hadn't wanted to tell Raymond that I was lost. He seemed so sure of his own way. I looked down to see if I could make out the animal path we had come on but there were a lot of different paths. The only thing I could do was to keep the sun on my right so at least I knew I was going south. I was pretty sure that was the way I had to go. I wound around for a while without seeing anything familiar or it all looked familiar so nothing stood out. I never came to the rocks. I started to think I should turn around and take a different path when I recognized the stand of trees I had come to much earlier in the day. Oaks. Great big oaks changing color. I almost didn't realize they were the same ones where I had seen the shadow. The afternoon light made everything seem so different. I wondered if Mama Bear and her cubs were still around and then hoped hard that they were not.

Turning away from the oak stand, I walked toward the sun guessing that would lead me back to the creek bed where I had started my journey. It seemed like it had to be right at the edge of the trees but it wasn't. The nice full feeling I had had after Raymond and I ate the chewy pink meat had disappeared and instead I had a nagging hunger that was making me start to feel pretty sorry for myself. Why couldn't I find that creek bed? My sisters must be desperately worried about me by now. I didn't imagine though that they would come looking for me especially with Maudie laid up the way she was. Pa would head out as soon as he knew I was missing but the day was not nearly far enough gone for that to happen. In fact, when I thought about it I was sure that Pa, Ma and my brothers would not be back from New Ulm until past dark. I was not feeling much like I wanted to be out wandering around after dark.

Crows cawed above me and the sun crept lower and lower. The warmth of the midday was fading into a late afternoon chill. I came to a big, fallen tree blocking my path. Thick branches stuck out in every direction. I walked from one end to the other but I couldn't make out where the downed tree stopped. The failing light had taken the edges away from things. That big tree just dissolved into the rest of the woods. And all of it seemed to crowd in around me in an unfriendly darkness. I sank down on the ground; my feet throbbed from a day of walking on acorns. I tried to think. Should I go back and find another path? Sit and hope Pa would come? The day that had stretched out before me not so long ago now shrank back in a gloomy way. Would Pa even be able to find me? And what about Raymond? He was home by now – wherever home was. And here I was alone…almost.

I looked down at my arm and saw the first mosquito. I had time to swat it before it got me but the next ones came too fast. I couldn't fight off the whole swarm which hummed around me in the gray air. But mosquitoes meant water! I studied that big tree as hard as I could. I either had to climb over it which meant scratching myself up pretty bad or I had to find a way around. I had to feel my way along it. I found the root end and figured I couldn't make it around. It was way too tall and tangly. I worked my way to the other end. The light above me got narrower and the blackness grew but

I could feel the branches getting smaller. Near the top of the tree there was a dip in the ground below me. A creek bed.

My creek bed. "Hooray!" I yelled at the top of my lungs but there were only the crows and the tree people to hear me. Unless mosquitoes have ears? I pushed my way through the branches. They slapped and clawed at me but I finally got free on the other side. Then I ran. I let my feet squish into the few muddy patches left by the recent rain. The coolness felt good on my sore feet. Once I took the last bend that ran along our property, I bolted toward the house. I half-expected to meet my sisters outside where they would be frantically waiting for my return but no one was there. The place was quiet. I could see light inside so I guessed they were in there stewing about my whereabouts. They had probably just gone back in when it had started to get dark. I felt bad that I made them fret and figured I would have to apologize for all the trouble. I knew I had better have that out of the way before Ma and Pa came home which would probably be pretty soon.

When I opened the back door to the house, I found my sisters not pacing the floor but sitting across from each other at the kitchen table playing cards. They didn't even look up when I walked in.

"What are you doin'?" I sort of shouted. I couldn't believe my eyes. How could they just sit there while I was out lost in the woods?

"What does it look like we're doin'?" Maudie said looking down at her hand of cards. She still had dried smudges of bright yellow paste all over her face.

"I just thought one of you might care that I spent the whole day lost in the woods!"

"You weren't lost," Mabel did finally look up at me – in that knowing way that big sisters have.

"Maybe he was. He has been gone a long time," said Maudie.

"I was lost and I came to an oak forest I've never ever seen before and I met…" I stopped. I wasn't sure if I wanted to tell anyone about my new friend Raymond. I had thought about it some but hadn't been able to decide whether I wanted to tell or not. On the one hand it made an awful good story, on the other hand talking about it was bound to change it somehow.

"Met who?" said Maudie.

"Whom," Mable corrected. Maudie stuck out her tongue.

"Not really met I guess but in a tree I saw a….bear..rrnn owl." I suddenly decided that if I wasn't going to tell anyone about Raymond I wasn't going to tell about the bear either. They had to go together.

"You saw a bearn owl? What's that?" Mable demanded.

"He means a barn owl. Don't you?"

"Yes! Up in a tree, I saw a big ol' barn owl."

"In the middle of the day?"

"Yup – broad daylight."

"Oh for Pete's sake! I don't believe a word of it." Mable was not convinced but I think Maudie either believed me or was just willing to go along with one more of my stories because she finally looked up and gave me a smile.

"I'm starving," I said partly because I wanted to change the subject but mostly because I was starving.

"We ate hours ago. You said you would be here." Mable said but then she softened enough to say, "There's a slice of bread with butter on the plate over there under the bowl. And you can have one of the apples from the basket."

I found the food and sat down at the table with my sisters. I practically swallowed the bread and butter whole and I ate the apple so fast it made my stomach hurt.

"Can I play cards with you?" They looked at each other. There was a long pause and then Maudie sighed and said, "All right. Your deal," and handed me the cards. The deck was one that she had gotten in her stocking the Christmas before. She was awful proud of those cards. Each one had a picture of a different flower on the back. They still worked okay though. The dealer got to choose the game so I picked rummy because I was really good at remembering all the cards that had already been played.

Later that night after our parents and brothers had come home and we had all had a late supper together, we were getting ready for bed when Mable said to me, "Were you really lost in the woods today?"

"Naw, I could never get lost around here."

"I didn't think so," she said.

The next day Pa had me help him repair a section of fence behind the vegetable garden. He often asked me to help him with chores like that. He set up two sawhorses and laid a long pine board on top. My job was to hold one end of the board steady while he sawed the other. Once he had the board just the right size, he had me hold it up while he nailed it in place. We had to do six boards In all Ie that's how big the bad place in the fence was. Pa was always having to repair one part of the fence or another.

We just about had our last board in place when I said to him, "Pa, have you ever seen a bear around here?"

"A bear? Around here? No, I have never seen a bear around these parts."

"What would you do if you did see a bear? Would you hide?"

"Hide? I don't know that that would do me much good. Bears have about the best sense of smell of any animal there is."

"They do? Could they smell you if you were all the way across a field from them?"

"Across a field?" He laughed. "They can smell something that's twenty miles away. That's what I've heard. What's all this about bears anyway? You goin' bear hunting?" He laughed again.

"No, I just thought I might like to see a bear some day that's all," I said all calm as if this news about bears had not made my heart leap up into my throat.

"Well," said Pa, "if you can bear with me a little longer we'll finish up this fence repair and then we'll go see if Ma can bear to let us have a piece of that apple pie she made this morning. What do you think?"

I laughed and said I would sure like a piece of pie. As we walked back up to the house together, I wondered to myself if Raymond's pa ever made silly jokes like mine did.

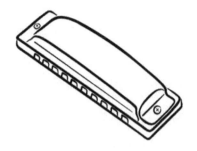

Chapter Three: The Floor Shook

I never remember Pa being so excited before. I never even knew adults got excited - in a good way that is. I sure knew they got excited in other ways - like how come there's a chicken on the loose, or why is the wood bin empty or can't you leave your sisters alone. But this was completely different. Pa was happy excited. Not that he wasn't usually a happy person. I guess you could say that's what he was. At least he was mostly cheerful; he hardly ever got mad and lots of times he made silly jokes. But for the last couple of weeks he had been whistling and chuckling and twirling Ma around the kitchen like they were at a dance. That made Ma laugh in a sort of embarrassed way. The whole thing was strange to watch - Pa all giddy like a little boy.

It had all started about two weeks before when we got this letter from Zanesville, Ohio. It was from Pa's older brother Vernon. Uncle Vernon was who my baby brother was named after only you'll remember that nobody but Pa called my brother Vernon. Everyone else called him Bunny. The letter said that the other Vernon, Pa's brother, was coming to see us. We didn't get too many visitors like that - from far away. Ma's parents, brother and her four sisters and their families came over often but they lived close by and so it wasn't the same. One time when I was little, the oldest son of a neighbor came to live with us while his sister had scarlet fever. His name was Per because his family was Norwegian. Pa said Per's pa was a really good dairy farmer but Ma was worried that me and my brothers and sisters might all get scarlet fever. In the end, she let Per sleep on the floor next to me anyway. He didn't sound Norwegian or anything and he said his sister's tongue was pink and looked like a strawberry. I guess she got better because he went home after a while and no one at our house got scarlet fever. Another time my Aunt Rosie's whole family had to spend the night because a blizzard came up while they were visiting and they couldn't even get their wagon back down onto the road. They left the next afternoon but it was crowded and noisy and fun while they were here.

The letter that came said that Pa's brother Vernon would be traveling by train from Zanesville to Sleepy Eye and would arrive on the Tuesday before Thanksgiving. Vernon was a brakeman for the railroad so I guess maybe he could take the train when he wanted to. He would be here in less than a week and Pa said our place should look its best for company. On the Saturday before the big visit, he put everyone, except Bunny, to work. Ma and my sisters cleaned the house from top to bottom. Floors were swept, mopped and waxed. Rugs were shaken and hung out in the cold November sun to air. I helped move furniture so they didn't miss any spots - although I was pretty sure Uncle Vernon wasn't going to go crawling behind the sofa to see if there was any dirt. All the sweeping, shaking and dusting filled the air with clouds of tiny specks that tickled my nose and made me cough and sneeze. I was sneezing up a storm when Ma said I should go outside and see if Pa needed my help.

Pa did have some jobs for me and the two older of my brothers to do. The little boys who were four and six were supposed to rake leaves and make a big pile. Pa would burn the stack of leaves once it was all raked up. Chilly, the six year old, was a pretty good raker. He worked carefully and patiently and didn't miss too many leaves. The rake was too long for him but he figured out how to hold it low down so he could get a good purchase on it. As far as I could tell Clayton who was two years younger just moved the leaves from one spot to another without there being much improvement. Pa didn't stop him though. I guess he figured it was better if Clay stayed outside and out of Ma's way. While the boys raked leaves, Pa and me worked on fence repair. There was always fence repair. Usually we worked on it a little at a time - just so no animals could get out - but now Pa wanted it all in good order before Uncle Vernon arrived. The worst spots were always on either side of the big shed that we called the barn. Our cow lived inside and we stored hay in the loft. I tried to avoid going in there since I had seen a ghost-sign of a swaying noose but I figured I was okay with Pa by my side.

Pa made a thick stack of the pine boards we were going to use and set up the saw horses. I did my usual job of holding the boards steady while Pa sawed. It was a raw day but working in the sun eventually made us so warm that we pulled off our jackets and hung them on a fence post. We could move around freer then and we made such good progress that by the time Ma called us in for dinner we had repaired the whole section of fence to the west of the barn. After dinner we would go back and finish the part to the east.

I hoped Uncle Vernon would notice our work because then he would be able to tell what a good team Pa and me were.

On the way up to the house Pa stopped to admire the giant pile of leaves that mostly Chilly had raked up, "That stack is going to put out an awful lot of heat."

Chilly hesitated as if to ask a question but then just smiled in his shy way.

"What is it Wilbur?" Pa liked everyone's regular name best. Chilly's was Wilbur. "Did you want to ask me something? Like could you jump in those leaves before we set them on fire?"

I didn't know how Pa knew that but Chilly nodded his head and Clay clapped his hands. I didn't say anything but I wasn't going to mind taking a leap into that pile either. We all went into the house and washed up. Ma had made the left-overs from a pot roast we had eaten a couple of days before into beef stew and boy did that smell good. Nobody talked as we ate our meal. We were too busy eating. Bread which has been slathered with butter and then has stew carefully stacked up on top - best to hold it over the bowl - is probably one of the most delicious foods in the world if you ask me. I generally ate it until I started to feel a little sick - then I knew I was full. On the other hand, I had to be sure I had room for pie. Ma was the best pie maker there ever was. My favorite was chocolate but I was happy with the raisin pie we had today. Ma poured steaming hot coffee into mugs for her and Pa. Sometimes Ma would pour me a saucer of coffee because she knew I liked to dunk my bread with jam and butter in it but just she and Pa drank it out of mugs.

Talking started up after the meal was over. Maudie wanted to know how long it was going to take Uncle Vernon to get here by train.

"A couple of days I imagine," was Pa's vague response.

"Don't you know how long it takes, Pa? Didn't you take the train here when you came?" Mabel asked.

"Me? No, I didn't. I didn't come straight here anyway. That's a long story."

"And we'd better not be telling it now when we have so much work to do," Ma stood up and started clearing dishes. Both my sisters got up as well. They couldn't very well sit there while Ma was doing up the dishes but I suspected that they were sorry like me not to hear the rest of the story.

"How about if after our work day is over, I tell you about how I came to Sleepy Eye?"

"Yes, Pa we really want to hear," Mabel spoke for all of us.

By the time we were back outside the sun had already started its descent toward the west. It was colder now than before dinner and the heaviness in the air suggested snow.

Snow was always a welcome diversion but I hoped nothing would stop Uncle Vernon from coming. I would be disappointed but worse still would be to see Pa's disappointment.

Pa and I worked another couple of hours on the fence. Pa was determined to finish what we had started before dinner. Chilly and Clay had had to take over some of my chores - pumping water and carrying armfuls of cookstove wood into the house. None of us took off our jackets now. Instead we pulled our caps down over our ears and raised our collars up around our necks. Still the chill crept in as the sun dropped.

Finally Pa said, "I think that's about all we can do for today. I can't see to cut anymore."

In the growing dusk, we gathered up tools and sawhorses. Pa called for Chilly and Clay to help us. On the way to the tool shed, we passed the big pile of leaves. Clay stopped. He just stood there with his short arms wrapped around Pa's level. Pa kept walking but when Clay didn't follow he turned around and saw him still standing by the pile of leaves.

"That's right. I forgot. You haven't had your run in the leaves. Come help me put this all away and you can have a few jumps. And what about your sisters? Do you think we had better count them in?"

As soon as I set down the sawhorse I had carried, I ran to the house. "Mable, Maude," I yelled at the doorway. "We're getting ready to jump in the leaves!"

Mabel came to the door carrying Bunny.

"Hurry! Pa's going to let us jump in the leaf pile before he sets it on fire."

"What am I supposed to do with him?" She nodded her head at our baby brother.

"How should I know? Give him a spoon to play with and set him on the floor. Hurry!"

"Don't forget to get Maudie," I added as I dashed back down the steps.

The five of us took turns. Chilly got to go first. That was only fair; he had been the one to make the pile to begin with. Then Clay. This was an honorary position as I doubt he had done much real raking. Then we went by age - Mabel, then Maude, then me. The leaves that had mostly fallen weeks earlier were no longer at their prime but that didn't stop our fun. We kept the rake handy because after every couple of jumps the pile sort of spread itself out. Pa helped. And when it got so dark we couldn't see the leaves well enough to rake them anymore, Pa took the last leap. We kids jumped up and down and laughed to see our old pa jumping into a pile of leaves. Then he lit the fire. It was all smoke at first because of the sogginess of the leaves but then it made a whoosh sound and burst into flames. The sparks flew up into the black sky like so many runaway stars. Ma came out with Bunny in her arms and all eight of us stood with our brightened faces turned toward the blaze.

Pa was true to his word about finishing his story. After supper that night we settled in close to the stove. The little boys were asleep. Bunny had been put to bed before we even sat down to eat and Chilly had just about fallen asleep during the meal. He had worked and played so hard all day that he could hardly keep his head from bobbing around. Ma sent him and Clay to bed which made Clay cry but Chilly didn't protest. I knew how Chilly felt. I was pretty tired myself but I wasn't about to miss Pa's story. After clean-up was finished, Ma sat down by the lamp with her knitting and Pa pulled out his pipe and a pouch of tobacco. Whenever he smoked his pipe it seemed to take him forever to clean it out, pack the bowl carefully with pinches of tobacco and then finally light it - or try to light it.

"You spend more time fooling around with that thing than you do smoking it," Ma said to him.

"It's all part of the pleasure of the enterprise," Pa said and then winked at us kids. I could never tell when he was serious or not when he said things like that. I suppose Ma couldn't either because she sort of sniffed and just kept looking down at her knitting.

After he finally got the pipe lit, Pa asked us kids, "Where do you want me to start?"

"Why did you leave your home in Ohio, Pa? Didn't you like it?" Mabel went first.

"Like it? I liked it fine I suppose. But there wasn't much work in them days for a young fella like me. I had to make my way in the world and that meant moving on."

"Where did you go first? And how did you get there?" I took a turn.

"We walked. It took us a few days but where we went was Lake Erie."

"Who's we?"

"Me and some other young fellas. We was looking for work and there was work along the Lake."

We three older kids knew about the Great Lakes from our geography lessons at school. We had had to memorize the name of each and be able to point on the big map where each one was.

"What did you do there at the lake?"

"We loaded and unloaded freight. There's a big port there in the city of Toledo. Busy place with lots of work."

"How come you left there Pa if there was so much work?"

"Have you heard of unions? Those are groups of fellas who get together to make sure they get paid right and don't get taken advantage of by big companies. Well, they have a union of longshoremen there in Toledo and they didn't much appreciate our working there without being part of their group."

"What's a longshoreman Pa?" I asked and Mabel sighed loudly to indicate that she already knew.

"That's a fella that loads and unloads ships."

"Where did you go next?"

"North. I went up past Lake Superior into the forests of Ontario."

"You walked all that way?!" Maudie asked.

Pa laughed, "No, I didn't walk all that way. Mostly, I hitched rides on wagons going north. I found work at a logging camp up there and stayed through the winter.

"Were you alone? What happened to the fellas you left with?"

"Oh, they stopped here and there along the way. They found steady work or thought they could. I was the only one who made it all the way into Canada."

"Were you lonely then Pa?" Maudie who was soft-hearted wanted to know.

"It was a desolate place alright. Nothing but trees and some men to take them down. And they weren't all too sociable those men up there and quite a few didn't speak English so not too many chances to make friends."

"What language did they speak then?" This was Ma's first question. I hadn't even been sure she had been listening. She had been so quiet and attentive to her knitting.

"Any number spoke French. A couple spoke Italian. Those two mostly stayed to themselves since they had each other to talk to. And one fella spoke Chinese."

"Chinese?!" We all three said at once. This was a very interesting development.

"How did a Chinese man get all the way up there, Pa?" I asked not really quite knowing where up there was. It did seem awful far from China wherever it was.

"He came across from Vancouver working on the railroad. I don't know exactly how he landed in that camp but he was a hard worker and didn't cause no trouble."

"Where did you live? In a tent?"

"A tent? No, it was terrible cold up there. I arrived at the beginning of winter - about this time of year. The foreman said cutting trees was easier in the cold when the sap wasn't running. There were some shacks that had been built before I got there. We didn't need much except a warm place to lie down in after a long day of work." He paused. I thought he was going to stop the story there but after he glanced over at Ma, he started up again.

"One day, me and two Scots were way out in the woods far away from camp. The foreman told us to go out along a ridge and fall a line of white pines. Later we would go back to roll them down the embankment toward the outer edge of the camp. The ones that didn't roll on their own that is," he laughed and then went on. "It had been a clear day. Biting cold but mostly sunny- not bad weather to work in. About mid-day though the clouds grew darker and the wind picked up. We all three knew it was going to snow and we had better get out of there in a hurry. We grabbed our tools and made a dash for it. But the snow came before we had gone even a quarter mile. It was slow going in that squall. One of them Scots was a big man and he was in an awful hurry to get out of the storm. He wouldn't wait for me or the other Scot. Instead he plunged on ahead by himself. Not one of us could see a foot in front of us. A whirling curtain of white lay between us and the rest of the world. Me and Bobby, I think the one Scot's name was, kept a steady pace. Every once in a while there was a lob tree to mark the trail."

"What's a lob tree Pa?"

"That's a tree that's had the branches cut off but hasn't been cut down. They mark the way in places where the trail is hard to find. Anyway, I think we might have made it only we came to this steep drop-off. We were lucky we didn't walk right over the edge but we had been walking slowly enough that we had spotted a lob tree beyond us to our left. The other fella hadn't been so fortunate. We could hear him yelling from somewhere on the slope below. It was a miracle we heard him at all the way the wind was blowing. He was raising quite a ruckus though - hard to miss. We had some rope and we let it out over the edge. He was able to get around himself and then gave the rope a hard tug. Like I said he was big. The two of us had quite a time getting him up."

"What did you do then Pa?"

"Was he hurt?"

"Did one of you go for help?"

"Hold on! I can't answer everybody at once. Let's see. Yes, he was hurt. He had twisted his ankle bad on the way down. We couldn't see any bones sticking out but it seemed likely it was broke."

"What did you do?'

"There was not much we could do. By the time we had him up top it was dark. There would be no more walking that night. Those thick snow clouds had completely blocked the moon. The only light was little flickers off the falling snow. We found the driest spot we could under a couple of big elms that hadn't quite lost all their leaves yet. We made a splint for the big fella's foot and rolled him onto a tarp that we had carried with us. Little by little we dragged him and the tarp under the elms. He made quite a fuss every time there was the least little jerk of the tarp but we got him there. Bobby gathered wood for a fire -there was plenty of dry wood under the leaves and brush - and I strung the tarp up with our rope. It wasn't much but it was better than nothin'."

"So you stayed all night in the woods?" It seemed to me that as Pa was telling us the story, the light from Ma's lamp had grown dimmer and the darkness of the room had become deeper. I almost got up to look out the window. I was so sure there would be snow.

"We did. It took us a while to get a fire going with the wind but we managed."

"Did you sleep?"

"Not a wink. I was afraid to fall asleep. Remember it was awful cold out. I didn't want to freeze to death out there. Bobby kept rubbing the big Scot so he didn't get too cold and I spent half the night on my feet. The ground was bone chilling. It was a long night."

"Where there wild animals?"

"Now that you mention it," Pa smiled as if he was just waiting to be prompted, "some time in the night that ornery wind finally dropped and the snow eased. Hard to know what time that was. I reckon after midnight. Without the constant roar I could make out a sound like a wail in the distance - maybe coming from the ridge we had logged. Then it was not just one wail but one then another and another. "Coyotes?" Bobby said. "No, it sounds more like wolves," was my answer. He didn't say anything else - just sank back against the elm trunk he'd been leaning on. But the wailing sounds let up pretty quick and I never heard them again. Besides clumps of snow falling from branches it was pretty quiet. The fire crackled now and then and the big Scot kept up his moaning. Hours went by and it seemed like it got even colder. Maybe close to dawn the snow stopped altogether and it was as still as a cat waiting to pounce. Then I heard a little rustle behind me and then I heard the same sound again. The second one sounded like it was out in front of me, then there was one to my left and one to my right. Bobby, who had been dozing, sat up straight and whispered, "Did you hear that?"

Straight ahead of us I could see two green balls shimmering in the blackness. The fire light didn't reach far enough for me to make out what it was but I knew all right. Two more came out of the darkness to my right, two on my left. I hardly dared to turn around to see behind but I made myself."

"Two more? Oh no! Pa"

"That's right. All those fearless green eyes staring right at us. We must have been surrounded. They say wolves will avoid a fire but they didn't avoid this one. Bobby was wide awake then and even the big Scot sat up. Then I heard a low growl. It was just barely loud enough to make out but Bobby heard it too and so did the big Scot. We thought them wolves had us for sure."

"I don't believe a word of it," Ma put in. That sure took the edge off the mood. I for one wasn't completely sorry though. I had begun to feel like our house was being watched by green eyes.

Pa laughed good-naturedly, "Well, I guess you had to be there, Liz."

"What happened then, Pa?"

"Did the wolves attack?"

"How did you get away?"

"Oh, we weren't too heroic I s'pose. We all three yelled our lungs out while me and Bobby pulled lit pieces of wood from the fire and threw them as hard as we could in the direction of those covetous eyes. It didn't take too long before them wolves scampered away one by one. Just one stopped and turned to gaze back before he disappeared with the rest. I don't suppose any of us looked too good to eat."

"Oh Pa!"

"That's enough stories now," Ma said, "time you all got to bed."

"But we didn't hear about the end of your journey here. How did you get from Canada to Sleepy Eye?'

"In the spring, one of the fellas at the camp told me about farms in Minnesota that needed hands. I figured I'd rather be a farmer than a logger any day. Now you'd all better do what your ma said and get to bed. No more stories tonight."

By morning, it really was snowing. I looked out of the window into the still darkened sky and could see the big flakes drifting disastrously down. But by the time I got out to do my chores I was relieved to find that the ground was soggy with melting snow that hadn't really stuck. I figured Vernon's train would have no trouble making it through a little slush.

Then the days dragged. On Monday, I barely heard what Miss Jordahl was saying - something about the first Thanksgiving maybe but all I could do was stare out the window and will the sky not to make snow. I kept trying to imagine what Uncle Vernon would look like. The only thing I could come up with was a fuzzy version of Pa. Then at long last Tuesday came and Pa said we didn't have to go to school because we would all go into town together to pick up our company. I could hardly believe it. It was almost like Christmas had already come. I figured Ma would stay home with Bunny but when it came time to climb into the wagon she was ready and all bundled up like the rest of us. I could barely see the baby - he was so buried in sweaters and blankets. All that poked out was his little nose and Ma smashed that up against her chest while we rode along so he wouldn't get cold there either. The day was damp and biting.

I watched the droplets of my breath collect in front of me. I liked to pretend I was smoking when I could see my breath like that. The trip into town took most of an hour. We would have made it faster only Chilly had to get out to pee on the way. I guess he hadn't listened to Ma when she asked everyone including Pa if they had been to the toilet. He had to take off almost everything he was wearing - Pa helped him - and then he had to put everything back on. He was shaking when he got back in the wagon. Mable had him sit in her lap so she could wrap her arms around him.

We still arrived at the train depot an hour and a half before Uncle Vernon's train was due. Pa hadn't wanted to take any chances. Ma sat down on one of the long wood benches in the warm station with Bunny. The rest of us wandered around looking at trains and watching people. I thought I could tell which folks were waiting to meet someone coming in on the train. They were the ones who seemed restless and impatient. Just like us! We all kept looking at the big station clock and down the empty track as if we could compel the train to arrive by the force of our unwavering attention. Then the energy of the crowd shifted and we could see that the 10:54 from Minneapolis was pulling into the station right on time. The huge cars seemed to defy the force of their forward motion. First they slowed and then they came to a stop with a loud squeal. Within minutes people were spilling out of their doors. Ma came out of the station and Pa walked along the cars tense and alert. I looked every which way to see if I could pick out my uncle but everybody was rushing by me so fast I couldn't really see their faces.

All of a sudden, Pa came to a stop. It was like he had seen a ghost or something. I suppose when you haven't seen your brother in so many years and you finally do, it must feel like you're looking at a figment of your own imagination. There he was and in my wildest dreams I wouldn't have conjured up Uncle Vernon. He must have been a foot taller than Pa - at least. Though that was the very least remarkable thing about him. More amazing was the way he was dressed. On his head he wore a stovepipe hat. I had never seen anyone wearing such a hat before but I knew what they were from photographs like ones of Abraham Lincoln. But this hat was nothing like Lincoln's because it bent in the middle like someone had dropped it or had stepped on the crown. Also this one had a long, colorful feather stuck in the band. I had never seen that in a photograph. Besides the hat was his coat which hung so far down on his body that it very nearly dragged on the ground. It was made of strips of mismatched fabric sewn together in long vertical columns. No one I knew had a coat like it. Strangest of all may have been a sort of tapestry shawl he had wrapped around his neck. The fabric made me think of a flying carpet from *Arabian Nights* and my uncle himself seemed to have stepped out of an exotic fable. I had never been to the circus but I had seen pictures. Uncle Vernon could have been ring master. Pa didn't seem to notice what his brother was wearing. He just looked him right in the eyes and then wrapped his arms around him. I had never seen grown men hug and it made me feel shy. Since I was standing right next to Pa, he introduced me first.

"This is my oldest boy Philip." Uncle Vernon reached out to shake my hand and I was glad that I came to myself enough to reach mine out in response. His grip was firm - not like some adults who seemed to think shaking hands with youngsters is a waste of time. Everyone in the family took a turn being introduced. I could tell by the looks on their faces that Uncle Vernon had made quite an impression on them as well - especially on Ma. Ma was a person who did not ordinarily wear her heart on her sleeve but I think it would be fair to use the word gaping to describe her expression when she saw her brother-in-law for the first time.

The ride home was boisterous - filled with countless questions being called out over the sound of horse hooves clicking against the ground. The returning answers added to the general uproar and it was impossible to follow the sense of it if there was any. How old were each of us? What grade in school? What subject did we like best? What was our teacher's name? These were pretty standard adult questions but our uncle asked us others. Did we like turnips? Or did he say trumpets? Either way the answer escaped me. Could we whistle? What tunes? Did we have a harmonica? Could we play "Turkey in the Straw" on it? No, we couldn't because we didn't own a harmonica. When he heard this he called back to us that he had one and he would teach us how to play. Besides his traveling bag which rode in the back with us kids our uncle had brought with a mysterious, small black case. I was curious about the contents of this case but hadn't really had the chance to have a good look at it. What could be in there? This fantastic looking man might have carried almost anything with him. Unfortunately he had not put the case in the back but was holding it in his lap.

The three adults sat on the bench seat at the front of the wagon - Pa on one side holding the reins, Uncle Vernon on the other and Ma in the middle. From the back she looked especially small next to our uncle. His tall stature, towering hat, and big coat dwarfed her so that she almost looked like a little girl. I think his very presence might have dwarfed her as well. His speech and demeanor matched his outfit exactly. I couldn't remember having heard a voice quite like his before - much deeper than Pa's but not loud. It was more of a rumble than a boom. And he carried himself in the most

unusual way. It was like he had always known us and he was
just as happy as could be to see us again.

Ma had made sure there would be a meal ready when
we got home. The hot food was welcome after our cold ride.
We sat around the table as we usually did - only we made
plenty of room for Uncle Vernon. He had shed his coat and
hat but he kept the shawl and I couldn't blame him because it
took awhile for the house to heat back up. Normally at meals
we didn't talk much when we were eating. It wasn't a rule or
anything - it just was our way and also the way of my
grandparents and most of my aunts and uncles and their
families. Eating was one thing and talking another. Uncle
Vernon seemed to have a different notion altogether. As
soon as we had our food he started in. He had a lot to say
about a lot of things - about the folks back in Zanesville,
about the train trip, about the look of the country from Ohio
to Minnesota, about the end of the war in Europe, about a
Tarzan movie he'd seen just before he came. The reeling out
of topics made my head whirl. Ma didn't seem to be able to
keep up either. She sat silent at her end of the table. Pa
though joined right in just as if breakneck conversation
around the table was the most natural thing in the world. And
in no way did Uncle Vernon leave us kids out. Just like during
the wagon ride he had a hundred questions. We hardly had
time to answer one before he asked another. What did we

think of the Red Sox winning the World Series? Did we think they could have done it without Babe Ruth? Who did we like better Douglas Fairbanks or Wallace Reid? What flavor of chewing gum is our favorite? At that time, I had only ever had Black Jack so that was my favorite.

When the meal was over Pa gave Uncle Vernon a sort of tour around our place- first the house. Ma had made a spot for him to put his things on the bottom shelf of a table in the hall. We had borrowed a roll-away for him from Ma's sister Rosie. For now it was tucked in the corner of the kitchen but tonight we would slide the table over and open up the bed. It had a quilt and a pillow mashed up inside so he would have everything he needed. Seeing him standing next to it, I had my doubts about how well he was going to fit but all he said was, "Thanks, Liz. That will suit me fine." When he got to the front room, he asked Pa, "Have you ever had any dances in here Oren?"

Dances? I'm not kidding! That's what he said. And the thing is he didn't seem to be kidding either. I am pretty sure everyone heard him say it because the house went silent. Even Pa was finally overcome. When Pa didn't answer, Uncle Vernon seemed to sense that we had not ever had any dances in our front room.

But he went on anyways, "We could just push the furniture up against the wall and roll up the rug. Me and Rhea have dances often. We could get maybe twenty people in here. Maybe a tight squeeze. Let's say fifteen to eighteen. How about Friday night?" He grinned. Rhea was Uncle Vernon's wife. I guess she was spending Thanksgiving with her own people. No one had said. It took Pa a minute to recover and then he said, "Let me think it over. What would we do about music?"

"I've got my fiddle with me and I expect we can find some others who wouldn't miss a chance to join in." That was it - the small, black case had a fiddle in it. I couldn't decide what I thought of a dance in our house. People had dances in their barns sometimes in the summer but I didn't remember anybody we knew having on right in their house. Maybe they did that in the big houses in town. I might not have known what to think but my sisters had no trouble at all.

"Can we Pa?" they said pretty much in unison. "Can we really have a dance?" Clay made a high-pitched squeal and jumped up and down clapping. Chilly smiled. Everybody else seemed to be smitten with the idea. Except Ma. She was silent and not smiling.

"Let us grownups talk it over," was Pa's noncommittal response. I figured that was the end of it. The outcome of grownups talking in my experience was usually, "No!"

After we kids had gone to bed, I could hear the grownups talking in the kitchen. The thing was I couldn't make out what they were saying. I could tell who was talking though and no surprise it was mostly Uncle Vernon. Talking and laughing. Pa talked some too. And maybe he laughed. I couldn't hear Ma's voice at all. That could have been because she spoke too quietly or she might have been waiting to talk to Pa alone. When I finally fell asleep they were still talking. But I woke again some time in the night. I hardly ever woke up before morning unless Bunny was crying or Chilly was jabbing me with his foot. It took a minute for me to realize what had woken me. It was a sound that came from the kitchen but it wasn't voices. It seemed so strange at first because I could have sworn I heard a train whistle. I loved the sound of trains. We lived too far from the tracks for me to hear them often but when we went into town or Pa took me on his rounds I couldn't wait to hear the long, low call of a passing train. I don't know why but somehow the sound was stirring to me. I slipped out of bed.

There was a stub of a candle on the very edge of the kitchen table. The light it cast was so weak that it reached no further than my uncle's dark shape on the edge of his bed. He was so much too tall for the height of bed that his knees came almost to his shoulders. His tapestry shawl was wrapped around his shoulders and he was blowing softly into a shiny silver harmonica. At least that is what I thought it was. The instrument was hardly visible; his big hands covered it almost completely. I stood there a minute before he spotted me. He didn't tell me to go back to bed. He didn't even stop playing. He just nodded at me and smiled with his eyes. I pulled back one of the kitchen chairs without making a sound and sat down. Uncle Vernon kept playing and I listened - then he whispered, "Would you like to learn how to play?" I did really want to give it a try but I said, "I think we might wake up the others?"

"Right you are. How about tomorrow then? Just you and me and the mouth organ?"

"Yes. Please."

The next day Pa took Uncle Vernon on his rounds and we four older kids went to school. About mid-morning it started to snow again - pretty hard this time so Miss Jordahl had us leave early. I wasn't a bit sorry. I didn't have to worry about the train making it through the snow any more and who doesn't like to get out of school early? We all flew out of the door and made our way half walking and half playing in the falling snow. By the time we got home, Pa and Uncle Vernon were also back. The Thanksgiving holiday was starting early. I did my chores as quickly as I could and then went to find where the two men were. I wondered if Uncle Vernon would remember about the harmonica lesson. I found them next to the barn admiring our fence repair. Pa gave me a lot of the credit and Uncle Vernon slapped me on the back pretty hard and said I was a "Cracker-jack fence repairman."

I traipsed after them while they walked around the place and talked. Just like always Uncle Vernon had about a million questions for Pa. "How many acres do you have in alfalfa? Is that what gets the best price around here? How many dairy farmers are on your route? Who has the biggest dairy in the county?" Pa did his best to volley back his answers but he no sooner answered one than it made Uncle Vernon think of another. They were so absorbed in the crossfire, I was beginning to lose hope for my harmonica lesson. Then Pa broke in, "You know what? I forgot to rinse out those milk cans we brought back. Why don't you and Philip head back up to the house where it's warm and I'll join you in a few minutes."

Naturally, Pa didn't know anything about a harmonica lesson. I think he just needed a break from Uncle Vernon's inexhaustible zeal. We might go a whole day in our family without anybody asking anybody else even one question. On the way back up to the house with Uncle Vernon I felt shy about bringing up the lesson but I figured if I didn't say something I'd miss my chance. "Do you think this might be a good time for that harmonica lesson?"

He stopped walking and turned. I was afraid he was going to slap me on the back again but he just said, "The perfect time." In order to be alone, we had to go back down to the barn. Uncle Vernon sat down criss-cross applesauce on the barn floor and I sat down on Ma's milking stool. It wasn't toasty warm but I didn't care about that. First Uncle Vernon showed me how to hold the harmonica in my left hand. He said that was because I'm right-handed. It went on top of my thumb and under my pointing finger. My hand didn't cover the harmonica like his but he said that didn't matter. Then he showed me the ten holes and explained how they made different kinds of sounds.

"You have to pretend you're giving the harmonica a big slobbery kiss," he laughed and then when he saw I wasn't laughing, said, "Or better yet eating a sandwich. Just pucker up."

I puckered up and blew. I couldn't believe how much like a real note it sounded. Then he showed me how to breathe in and breathe out. It mostly got better each time I tried. Uncle Vernon just sat there and reminded me of what to do while I played.

"Don't just fill up your lungs with air." "Wet your lips." "Let it out slowly."

I tried my best to do everything just like he said. I played and he listened. I don't know how long we were there but when Pa came to find us he said supper was ready.

"Well, how do you like the harmonica?" my uncle asked.

"It's fun," I said. "Thank you for teaching me." Except for paper kazoos Miss Jordahl had us make once I had never in my whole life played an instrument before and now I had had my first lesson on the harmonica.

The day after Thanksgiving we had a dance in our front room. Uncle Vernon played the fiddle. He didn't wear his coat or shawl but he did have on his stovepipe hat with the feather in it. Mr. Miller, a dairy farmer on Pa's route, played the banjo and our neighbor Mrs. Bertrand played the accordion. The musicians showed up early before the guests arrived. Pa and Uncle Vernon had already moved most of the furniture out and had rolled up the rug. I kept waiting for Ma to make a fuss about the sofa or the rocking chair or something but she was too busy. She and her sisters and their ma were all in the kitchen piling food on big platters. There was lots of ham and turkey leftovers from Thanksgiving besides that there were thick slices of bread, every kind of pickle you can think of and a big pot of baked beans which I had been smelling for hours. Later when the guests came, every household brought even more food. Eventually there would be enough food to feed the county. Ma and the others brought out the platters and put them on a table that we almost never use. It always has a big doily on it with a fancy bowl in the middle. Someone had taken the bowl and doily off and had moved the table up against the wall. There wasn't nearly enough room on that one table for all the food so they had to leave some of the platters in the kitchen. When people started arriving most of the men went right through the front room and out the front door. Then they stood outside in the cold. The women went into the kitchen with their food and stayed in there until there was no more room. We kids moved among the crowd as best we could.

The music was sort of in the background at first. Nobody seemed to want to be the first out on the floor. More men drifted outside where someone had opened a jug of cider. Each man took a turn taking a pull on the jug and then handed it to the next person. Mabel and me sat down on the porch swing so we could watch the men drink and smoke. The music drifted out but no one paid much attention. Then Ma's sister Rosie stuck her head out of the door and said, "Any of you folks want something to eat?" It was like Miss Jordahl dismissing school but instead of a rush for the outside there was a rush to get in. Everyone smashed in around that one little table. It reminded me of how Pa showed me a hive of bees swarm once. Instead of a whole lot of separate little beings they all became one oozie thing. For a few minutes I couldn't even see the table - just bodies pushing to get in.

The food changed everything. It didn't even seem to be that people were that hungry. Quite a few left their plates half-finished when they went out to the dance. They just needed the food to get started. Couples, singles, old folks and kids all spilled out onto the floor. The musicians responded by stepping up the tempo and the volume.

Besides playing the fiddle Uncle Vernon also called the dance. That meant that he yelled out what the dancers were supposed to do. Some people seemed to know what to do already and some people just did what they wanted no matter what Uncle Vernon said. Sometimes the dancers went crisscross and sometimes they marched down a long row of other dancers. No matter what they did every single person had a big smile and not a few were out right laughing. More than one adult who normally behaved like life was pretty serious business actually threw their head back and howled. It was quite a sight.

Pretty soon a group of older kids broke away from the rest of the crowd and made a circle of their own in the middle of the floor. They joined hands, raised their knees way up, kicked and slapped their feet hard on the floor. Uncle Vernon and the other musicians loved it. They started to play at a furious pace. I guess it was what they call hillbilly music - like the kind Uncle Vernon could play on his harmonica. I didn't know the names of any of the tunes but they were all hand-clapping and foot-stomping. And that's what people did. Uncle Vernon stopped calling out directions and the circle in the middle grew and the music got faster and the clapping got louder. Even the spectators were stomping their feet. Pretty soon the whole floor started to shake and I watched as the large photograph of my grandparents that hung on the wall slid over to one side. A mug someone had left near the edge of the table bounced right off and fell on the floor. I saw it happen but I couldn't hear the sound of breaking china over the roar of the music. My sister Maude grabbed my hand and we wiggled our way into the crowd of dancers. There was so little room all we could do was jump up and down to the beat of the music. It made me laugh just like everyone else but I don't know why. I looked at Maude and she was laughing and all the way across the room I could see that Ma was laughing too. We all laughed into the night while the music played and the floor shook.

In the morning Pa went alone into town to take Uncle Vernon to his train. I asked to go along but Pa said not this time. I guess he wanted it to be just him and his brother. Later when Ma was pulling the blankets off the bed where Uncle Vernon had been sleeping she found a small package with twine around it. "To Philip" was written on the paper wrapping so she gave it to me. I took it outside where I could open it by myself. It was the harmonica.

Chapter Four: Hopes and Fears

The snow that had fallen the day before Thanksgiving stuck. It wasn't much but it lasted. Once I had stopped worrying about Uncle Vernon's train travel I was glad to see the snow stay around. I know Ma and Pa, and no doubt every other adult in the county, was sorry to see the snow come that early, but there is not a boy in the world who does not love snow. There is something about snow that is so cheering. It could be its whiteness. Usually when snow first falls the world is pretty drab. The trees are leafless and the fields have long been harvested. There is a starkness that the snow brightens. There is also the fact that snow falls. Rain falls, of course, and is all right up to a point. If I play out in the rain I can get soaked in no time. Adults generally are against children staying out in the rain.

If I am playing in the rain, Ma will call, "Philip Stanley, you get in here this instant. You're going to catch your death a'cold."

There must be some evidence for this kind of warning but I myself have never known any boy, or anybody else, who has caught his death a'cold from playing in the rain. It might be the playing part that makes all the difference. Maybe if you are working in the rain with all those cold drops rolling down inside your collar and soaking into your undershirt, maybe you do catch a cold. But if you are running and jumping and sliding, you do not seem to suffer so much from the rain. I don't think Ma remembered this from her own childhood but then that was a very long time ago.

Snow is entirely different from rain. It falls but it does not get a person so wet all at once. A boy can be out in the snow for hours and hours and no parent will scold him or try to stop him. He may actually get as wet as can be but the wetness of snow is not generally thought to cause colds so he is left alone.

And so it snowed and I was happy. A few days before Christmas, the snow came down in those big, flat flakes that really stick together. They can easily be made into a snowball or, if there is enough, into a fort. That day in December there was not really the right amount of snow for a decent-sized fort but we decided to make one anyway. Maude and Mabel and I worked on that fort for most of Saturday morning after our chores were done. The two little boys had been sniffling and Ma was making them stay inside. Of course, my baby brother was not allowed out though I could see him and Ma standing at the window so he could see snow falling. He pointed at the flakes. He pointed a lot at that time.

In order to make a fort, we started with snowballs and made them bigger and bigger and then flattened them out until they were like snow bricks.

"They don't need to be fancy," I told my sisters, " Just keep making one after another."

"They're too heavy," Mabel warned. "It's going to collapse."

"I think it will be alright," Maudie said to make me feel better but not with much conviction. And it did not look promising. The individual snow bricks were smushed up against each other haphazardly and the whole roofline pitched to one side in an alarming way.

"We need water," Mabel insisted. "We can slather the water on and it will freeze until they're stuck good."

"It isn't nearly cold enough!" It was probably cold enough and it was a pretty good idea but sometimes you have to stand your ground when it comes to older sisters.

"It's going to collapse."

It did collapse. And so we had to start all over again. This time we used water, and we got it good and wet, but in the end we had a fort that we could go in and out of only if we crawled in on our bellies. I was the only one who went inside.

Later in the day, when the sun was warmer, Ma let us take the two little boys, who were driving her to distraction, and some old cardboard boxes over to the Gundersons' farm down the road. Their property had a little rise that they let us slide down in the winter. It wasn't much of a hill and there wasn't all that much snow but the sun had warmed up what there was and it was slick. Even though the hill didn't amount to much and was nothing like the great sledding spot near the lake, there was one part at the very end that first got steep and then rose back up like a saucer. If you didn't have sufficient speed you ended up inside the saucer and then you probably had snow down your collar and inside your boots which was fun enough but better still was getting up speed at the top so you could power through the saucer and then fly over the lip and come down on the other side. Bam! You either landed with the cardboard under you still spinning or you and the cardboard parted company and you were on your bottom spinning. Either way it was a good ride.

My sisters screamed throughout. As soon as they got to the top of the rise they started giggling. Once on their way they continued to giggle but added some high-pitched screams. By the time they got to the saucer there was just one long howl. Then they were back up on their feet, marching back up to the top, with more and more giggling on the way. They were having an awful good time but they were going to be worn out by the time we got home.

My problem was that I always had to take one of the little boys with me. You might think this was an advantage, because of the extra weight, and you would be right - to a point - but only to a point. The disadvantage was all the squirming. Those boys could really squirm and the squirming got worse on every run. The first time down each one sat stock still with fear and anticipation. But after the fear wore off, they couldn't keep still - especially Clayton who was only four. I didn't even take him to the top of the hill. Ma would have had my hide if anything had happened to him so I started halfway down. Like I said, the first run worked fine. He sat with his mouth hanging open and his hands gripping my legs as hard as he could. He couldn't quite reach to the sides of the cardboard sled.

"Ouch! Clay get your nails out of my thighs! Leggo!"

I don't think he could even hear me. He was so excited. I had to pry his chubby, little fingers open. I told him to grab hold of my pants which he finally did and then down we flew - not fast enough to make it through the saucer but fast enough to feel the cold wind on our cheeks and get our hearts pumping. Chilly was next. They took turns. Mabel and Maude refused to take them. They were too scared one of them would get hurt. It didn't seem to matter that I might be the one who got in trouble. Anyway I think the boys wanted to ride with me so down we went over and over again. And every single time I had to tell them to stop that squirming.

"No," I said. "You can't ride with me; you move around too much. I ain't going to take you any more."

"Please, Phil, please. I won't move. I promise. I'll just sit. I promise. Please take me." Chilly said. Clay just said "Please, please, please."

All that begging was hard to resist. But they never kept their word. Not once. We sledded all afternoon until the sun started to go down. When we got home, Pa was there and you could tell he wished he had been with us. Pa loved a good ride down the hill. I was sorry too because those little boys would have ridden with him instead of me.

"Well now," said Pa "once the lake is completely frozen over we can go out for a skate on the ice."

"Can we go tomorrow, Pa?" Maudie asked.

"No," he laughed. "Not tomorrow but soon."

The ice had been collecting on the lake. I was itching to get out there to see if it was thick enough to skate on,

In the Minnesota River Valley where we lived, every winter it gets to freezing and below. But some winters are colder than others. This one was one of those. In October, when the first snow flurries fell, the temperature at night fell to near zero. Besides the ice on the lake, there was frost on Ma's cabbages and squash. We spent one hurried morning harvesting the last of vegetables. The squash would keep with the potatoes, carrots and onions in the root cellar but most of the cabbage Ma made into sauerkraut which made the house stink to high heaven all day but tasted good later.

October had been just the beginning. Month after month it grew colder. By the first week of December, the lake was frozen all the way across - not a record but still early. The ducks were gone and the fish had gone deep. You could still fish on the lake if you made a hole in the ice - near shore at the beginning of winter but later you could go right out in the middle to make your hole. Once you sawed open a nice round circle - about two feet across - you could drop your line and bait right in and get a fish. Up north, some people even built little sheds on the lake so they could ice fish all winter.

Me and my sisters liked to skate out on the lake when the ice got thick enough. We screwed the blades onto the bottom of our leather shoes and slid out across the frozen water. We all three were expert skaters but there are really two types of skating. One is gliding along and making patterns in the ice. Sometimes it was fun to twirl around with another person - one of my sisters or more likely one of my friends. The other kind of skating is all about speed. I could skate fast and that's what I loved to do. Me and some other boys might get up a game of shinny. This was a kind of hockey but not so formal. We might use brooms or even fallen tree branches for the sticks. Some boys shaped a flat piece of wood so that it had a curve at the bottom, that worked best, but we used whatever was at hand. Anything the right size would work for a puck - usually a chunk of wood. The goals were also makeshift, a pile of snow or a row of rocks. The game was fast-paced and could be fierce with boys flying in every direction and the puck crashing into snow banks on either side. Mostly we didn't keep score and the game lasted as long as there were boys to play.

After a day of skating we came home with red, chapped cheeks and hands that were nearly frost-bitten. The warmth of the house made my fingers throb so that I could hardly stand it. But Ma heated up some hot cocoa for me and my sisters and we sat by the kitchen stove, sipping and warming up. Sooner or later, though, we had to stir ourselves for the evening chores. The wood stove box needed filling, the animals needed tending to and supper was not yet on the table. I was always in charge of the wood. Boy, was it hard to make myself go back into the cold which was now even colder than when we had been on the lake. Also cold feels much colder when you are gathering wood than when you are skating. But out into the dark evening I went. Far above me, glassy points of stars were breaking through the sky here and there and I stopped with my arms full of wood and looked up at the winter sky. Even in that aching cold I couldn't make myself look away.

Christmas - my favorite holiday - was on its way. The anticipation was almost painful. I guess mostly the adults did the work and the kids did the anticipating but everyone seemed to get a little jollier as the twenty-fifth grew closer. A couple of days after the building of our ramshackle snow fort, Pa offered to take Ma into town to do errands. It was the school holiday so the whole family got to go. While Ma and Pa did their errands, we five older kids walked around town. Nearly every shop on Main Street had set up a holiday scene in its front window. It was a winter wonderland. There were little villages topped with mounds of white cotton and Santas with eight tiny reindeer flying over miniature houses. In one store window there was a life-size Christmas tree with wrapped presents underneath. On either side was a child mannequin reaching out to decorate the tree. The general store had a real drum set and dolls all dressed in red and white. There were teddy bears too. One big one was riding a trike. My favorite window was the one in Kuske's Drug Store. They had set up the entire track for a Lionel train set. The train kept winding its way through snow-covered trees and up over a trestle and down again past a frozen pond. There was an engine, a caboose and coal cars overflowing with shiny black cubes. Through the windows of the passenger cars I could even see people looking back at me. The backdrop behind the track had been made to look like a snow-capped mountain. The mountain ledges had been filled with things they sold at Kuske's - blue bottles of Milk of Magnesia, Wild Cherry Cough Drops and boxes of Dr. Scholl's Foot Remedy. I was surprised at how pretty those things looked when they were balanced on the face of a snowy mountain.

While we were standing in front of Kuske's, a group of carolers gathered just to one side of the door. There were about twelve singers - mostly adults but there were a couple of older kids too. All of them were bundled up. It was cold. They sang "Joy to the World" first which was a good peppy carol to get started with. People stopped to listen and a few sang along. I hoped Ma and Pa would come along while the carolers were there.

Some people were calling out requests for carols. I had a couple in mind but wasn't thinking I wanted to say anything out loud when right next to me Mabel spoke up and asked for one. It was *O Little Town of Bethlehem* which is a good one but I never understood what the line "the hopes and fears of all the years are met in thee tonight" meant. I would have thought that Halloween was the holiday for fear - not Christmas. When Pa and Ma finally came the carolers were singing *Silent Night*. By then everyone in the crowd was singing along. I could hear my parents behind me join in. I thought the words from the carol "radiant beams" described that moment exactly.

At our place, Pa was in charge of the tree. Very early on Christmas Eve morning he slipped away with his ax and some rope and headed into the woods. We never saw him go and we had no idea where he kept the tree until it miraculously appeared in the front room. Ma was the one who decorated the tree with white candles set in little metal cups which were clipped onto the longest branches. There were also strings of dark red cranberries and glittery tinseled garlands that caught the light of the candle flames. The effect was otherworldly. We kids could hardly catch our breaths when we first saw it. I could sit for ages and just watch the light dance.

After our Christmas Eve supper and a last wistful look at the tree, we went to bed. Sleep was hard to come by. I only managed it by running some of the Christmas carols I had heard in town through my head over and over. For the last couple of weeks, I had been working on *The First Noel* on the harmonica Uncle Vernon had given me. I guess you could say it was coming along but so far no one in the family had been able to identify the tune when I played it. I tried to concentrate on it now so that it would distract me from all my wonderings about what might be waiting for me in my stocking. I had been hinting pretty strongly around my parents that a pocket knife would be just the right thing.. I didn't have much evidence that they had been convinced. I suspect Ma thought I was too young but Pa sometimes even said to me, "If you had a pocket knife you could...." So maybe he could talk Ma into it. I was afraid to think it though because if it wasn't there then I would be disappointed. The last thing I wanted was to be sorry for anything on Christmas.

In the morning one of Pa's socks would be filled with some kind of goodies for each of us. There would for sure be sweet and juicy oranges. I had never been to the tropics. I had never been outside of Minnesota - or even the Minnesota River Valley, but to me oranges tasted like the tropics looked in pictures in the *National Geographic Magazine*. Palm trees and warm, sandy beaches. Also there would be candy including a

cane of striped red and white which lasted all day. We sucked
the straight end to a sharp point and then, when the curved
part was small enough, shoved the rest into our mouths and
crunched on it until our teeth ached. The bottom of the
stocking would likely hold a small toy - a new rubber ball or,
in my case, it might be a small tin truck or there just might be
a pocket knife. And Ma probably would have knit us a new
pair of socks or mittens and put that in our stockings too.
Imagining that stocking bulging with possibility was nearly as
fun as emptying it on Christmas morning. Whatever else it
held, to me it was filled with the magic of Christmas.

We weren't much of a Santa Claus family. I mean by
that that the only two people who thought Santa put gifts in
our stockings were Chilly and Clayton. I was surprised that
Chilly kept believing that when he had watched Ma himself
knitting the mittens that ended up stuffed inside the leg part
of his stocking. I guess he just liked thinking there was a
merry old Santa who was loaded with a bagful of goodies. It
was a tempting image but I hardly could remember a time
when I believed in Santa. Whenever it was, my older sisters
soon filled me in on the real story. That's the kind of thing
big sisters do. But I didn't mind it at all. I was just as happy,
or happier maybe, to know that our parents had been the
ones to fill our stockings.

I finally fell asleep but it hardly seemed any time at all before I was awake again. It wasn't the fragrance of bacon frying for our Christmas breakfast that woke me up though it was a smoky smell. There were noises too. Muffled sounds of someone running. Sleep kept pulling me back but the sounds were insistent. A door slammed somewhere and I thought I heard Ma's voice. It seemed far away like an echo at the bottom of the cistern. But then I heard Pa's voice and it was closer and starkly clear.

"You get them out of the house. Grab blankets and shoes." The bedroom door shot open and smoke poured in. The smell was overpowering - hot, metallic and bitter. All of a sudden, Ma was standing over me.

"Get down on the floor," she said. I had never known Ma to be afraid but right then I could hear the fear in her voice. When I didn't move right away she grabbed my arm and pulled me off the bed onto the floor.

"Keep your head down," she said. "Don't stand up. You need to get out of the house."

Then her hand was gone. I was on the floor next to the bed and everything around me was black. I couldn't see what was in front or beside me. I understood that I had to move through the smoke-filled darkness on my hands and knees but I could not get my bearings - nothing seemed familiar in the house I had always lived in. All I could think to do was crawl forward until I came in contact with something and then turn. At first I tried to turn always in one direction but then I had the terrifying realization that I had been going in a big circle. While I tried to make my way forward, the menacing smoke became even thicker. It stung my eyes and burned my nose. It made me gag just to try to breathe. I strained to hear something - Ma or Pa calling or one of my brothers or sisters crying out but all I heard was a strange hum. It sounded like the smoke itself was vibrating.

I needed to stop and lie down for just a minute - until I could catch my breath. I was reaching forward to stretch out and let myself rest when I felt something cold roll over my hands. At first I thought there was a puddle of water on the floor but then I realized it was air. Cold air was streaming over my hands. Still fighting for breath, I forced myself back up on my hands and knees and crawled as fast as I could in the direction of the flowing air. I came to what I recognized was our back door and pushed it as hard as I could. The rush of air was sweet and icy. I filled my lungs with it.

Then I heard a voice I had been pining for. Ma called out, "Over here Phil! We're over here."

Everyone but Pa was huddled together in the yard. Ma and the girls were wrapping the three little boys in blankets. I was freezing. I realized then that I was standing in the snow in my bare feet. Mabel came up and put a blanket around my

shoulders and pushed an old pair of Pa's boots at me. I slid
my feet into them and turned to look back at the house.
Black billows of smoke rolled out of the open door and out
of somewhere on the roof. I couldn't see any flames. And I
couldn't see Pa. I was afraid to ask where he was. What if he
was inside looking for me? I didn't think I could stand that.

Before I had time to steel myself to ask about Pa, Ma
put a hand on each my shoulders, gave me a hard look and
said sharply, "Run to Bekkes' and call for help!" Bekkes were
our closest neighbors who had a phone.

I knew if I went around back of the chicken house and
through the stand of oaks it would take me only a few
minutes. I wasn't sure though how fast I could move in Pa's
boots.

I had to ask first, "Where's Pa?"

"Don't worry about him. He went in to get furniture
out before it's too late. Now run!"

I ran the best I could but I stumbled in the boots and
slid down onto the snow. I got up and ran again. Once I got
the hang of running in the boots I took the blanket off my
shoulders and held it in my hands so I could run faster. But
no matter how fast I ran I didn't seem to get anywhere. I
could still hear the hum behind me but I was afraid to look
back.

I made it almost to the edge of our property but still had to cross a long alfalfa field which Pa had harvested a lifetime ago. I made better progress in the field though than I had in the woods. I could run between the stubbled rows.

When I finally reached Bekke's property there were no lights on. I had no idea what time it was but it must have been before milking time. I tried pounding on the front door but that did no good so I went around back. Their dog, Jupiter, went crazy when he heard me and set up such a commotion that someone was at the door in seconds. It was Mr. Bekke. He opened the door and before I had finished my sentence, "Our house is on fire," he was on the phone. As soon as he had made the call and hung up the receiver, he told me to jump into his truck. The Bekkes liked all modern conveniences. Besides the phone, Mr. Bekke had had a motorized truck even before Pa had - and Pa had had one of the first in the county. I was in the truck with my blanket wrapped around me but there was no Mr. Bekke. I thought of jumping out and running back home when he did finally appear - carrying a bucket and an ax. I didn't want to seem smart so I didn't say anything about the size of the bucket versus the size of the fire. The ride back to our house was going to take longer than my run over. The Bekke's drive angled off in the opposite direction from our house and picked up a county road that was almost a half a mile away. I would have asked him to let me out so I could run back only my nightshirt was soaked through and the blanket which I had dragged in the snow was not much drier. I was awful cold and had started to shake.

Mr. Bekke reached over behind the seat and pulled out an old lap rug. "Here," he said "you better warm yourself up."

It seemed to take forever to get to our road and when we finally turned down it, my heart sank. I could see our house through the trees and the clouds of smoke had been replaced by shooting flames. There wasn't a door or a window that did not have fire leaping out of it. When we turned into our drive we could see that the pump wagon was coming up behind us. Mr. Bekke pulled up next to the corn crib in order to give the firefighters plenty of room. Men who had been hanging onto the side of the wagon now jumped off even before the driver had let it come to a complete stop. It took two of them to pull off the giant hose.

I recognized most of the firefighters. Many of them were really just farm boys like me only older. A few had come from town. All of them were volunteers who came ready to put their lives at risk for a neighbor they might only barely know. They swarmed over the place in a strangely efficient way. Their methodical movements contrasted starkly with the chaos of our burning house.

Flames made a sinister glow over our yard where pieces of furniture had been scattered here and there. A rocking chair rested up against the side of the chicken hutch, a chest of drawers sat cockeyed next to the cistern, Bunny's crib was anchored in a snow drift, and our kitchen table guarded the path to the barn. My sisters and brothers were still huddled with blankets around them but since I left they had pulled chairs up into their tight, little circle.

Ma yelled for them to get out of the way of the firefighters, "Move them chairs! They have got to get up to the house. Go over there by the barn." I helped them drag the furniture further away from the house. That warmed us up a bit but the cold was sinking in and everyone was shivering - especially the two little boys and the baby.

I said to Mabel, "Take the little boys and get into the cab of Mr. Bekke's truck. I can move the rest of the chairs."

She took Clayton by the hand. Maudie had the baby in her arms and the four of them walked off toward the truck. Chilly wanted to stay with me. The two of us moved the last of the chairs and whatever else we could lift into the barn. After that we wandered back into the yard and got as close we could to the house without getting in the way.

I hadn't seen Pa yet and I was silently praying, as well as I knew how, that he was not still in the house. Then I caught sight of him just at the edge of the ring of ragged light that lay across the yard. He was hunched over and coughing as if he could not stop. Ma stood next to him with a cloth in her hands. Whenever he could manage a short pause in his coughing, she would hold the cloth under his face so he could spit into it. Once I got close enough I could see that drool foamed out of his mouth onto a once white cloth that was now flecked with fearful black specks.

Ma saw me staring. "Your pa is all right. You better get him out 'a here." She nodded her head at Chilly who I had forgotten by my side. He was trembling in the frigid air. But I had no good idea where I should get him to. I took him by the hand and the two of us made our way back to Mr. Bekke's truck. In order to avoid the firefighters, we had to go around behind the pump wagon and when we came out at the far end we could see that all kinds of other people had arrived. The Gundersons had pulled their wagon up in front of the barn and other neighbors had come either on foot or on horseback. Both women and men had already set to work. Some were carrying buckets of water, others were moving the bigger pieces of furniture further away from the house.

Mrs. Bertrand had Bunny in her arms and was holding Clayton by the hand. When she saw me and Chilly approaching, she called out, " Phil, you let your ma know I've got the girls and these little ones. I'm gonna take them back to our place. and get them out of this cold. You understand?"

I nodded.

"You want to come too? And what about Wilbur? Better let me take him."

I wasn't going anywhere until I knew how Pa was but I figured Ma would want Chilly to go. I handed him off to Mrs. Bertrand. She turned and walked back to her wagon, piled everyone in and started off to her place.

Then I stood by myself and watched while our house burned.

Chapter Five: Sober Trunk

Pa was all right - at least for the time being. Our house was gone though. The firefighters had done their best. A faulty chimney they thought. The fire had been too far along when they arrived but Pa had saved most of the furniture. No one knew what happened to our Christmas stockings. They were probably part of the slurry of charred wood, scraps of scorched cloth, ashes and water that swam over the floor of what had been our home.

No adult seemed to give much thought to the missing stockings. Ma did dig around until she found some of the

Christmas tree candle holders. She put these away in a box filled with cotton until next year. That seemed like a long way away.

When the fire was completely out, all the helpers gone and the furniture stored in the barn, Ma, Pa and I got in our wagon and drove to Bertrands' where we gathered up the rest of our family. From there we headed out to my grandparents' house where we sat around their heavy oak table and ate a cheerless Christmas dinner. Nobody talked much except Bunny who babbled on making sounds that seemed like words but weren't quite. From that day on our family would not live together for many months.

My sisters stayed with our grandparents. The two girls were all they could manage and even that would be a stretch. Pa, Ma and the three little boys moved in with Ma's sister Rosie. They were an even greater hardship for my aunt and her family.

That left me.

Mr. Bertrand told Pa he admired the way I had run for help and kept my cool.

"A steady boy like that would be good to have around the place," he said when he offered to take me in. Pa and Ma were grateful for his generosity. I guessed I was lucky to have a place.

The Bertrands had five children. The older three were girls and the two baby boys were twins. The oldest girl had already left home to work for a family over in Mankato. She did some sewing and housekeeping and looked after the children. She came home every weekend and did the same things there. Her name was Ruth and she had long, yellow hair that she did in braids that wrapped around her head. Little wisps of gold always stuck out everywhere which made her look like she had a halo. She had blue eyes and when she smiled I could see her straight white teeth. I liked when she smiled.

When she came home on weekends, Ruth slept in a bed with her sisters and their German grandmother. Oma couldn't have taken up much room. She was smaller than my ma and my ma was pretty small. She might have been bigger - Oma that is - at one time but she had shriveled down to the size she was now. She was extremely shriveled. Oma apparently spoke no English but that did not stop her from talking. She talked or more like muttered almost all the time in German. Only Mr. Bertrand knew enough German to really speak with her although everybody in the family could recognize a few words.

"Der Eintopf ist zu salzig," Oma would declare standing over the kettle and Mrs. Bertrand would roll her eyes.

Mrs. Bertrand met every German word spoken by her mother-in-law with a complete disdain that amounted to righteous indignation. "This is America Oma. Speak English!" But the more Mrs. Bertrand complained, the less Oma seemed to understand.

I was given a bed in the "extra room" which was not quite a room - and not quite a bed. There was a space behind the stairs that went up to the attic where the girls and Oma slept. In that space Mrs. Bertrand had put a cot and a small table. On the wall opposite where I slept there was a high, little round window that I could look out of when I was lying down but that I could not reach when I was standing. When I lay on the cot the stairs were right behind my head so I had to be careful to remember to climb out before I stood up. Oma had made a big bag filled with duck down for my cover and it was the warmest thing I had ever slept under but the duck feathers sometimes stuck through the bag and scratched me in the night.

The Bertrands' house had electricity but my place under the ladder did not have any light so Ruth found a kerosene lamp and set it on the table. I read pretty well by then so each night I lay awake for a while and read a book by the light of the lamp. I was careful not to do it for long because I didn't want to have to ask Ruth for more kerosene. Lately I had been reading this story about a kingdom under the sea where there were fairies and mermaids and a shy octopus and lots of other good things. Miss Jordahl had told me to be careful of it when I took it home because it had some fancy pictures in it. Now I didn't know when I would get the chance to return it.

I didn't go back to school right away after Christmas vacation was over. That winter was so cold and snowy that school did not start right up again. Once it did it was too hard for me to get there. Only one of the Bertrand girls was school age. That was Mary. She was eleven but she had had scarlet fever and was not strong enough yet to go out in the winter cold. Helen, who was between Ruth and Mary, was done with school. She still lived at home and helped her ma with the housework and the babies most days. On the other days, she went into town and worked at the candy counter at Kuske's Drug Store. A farm girl like her was awful lucky, her ma said, to get a job in town. Most jobs in town went to girls from there but Mrs. Bertrand's brother was married to a Kuske so he helped Helen get the job.

Her pa had to drive her into town on the days she worked, which he didn't mind he said because he could do errands. Sometimes her ma went too. Nobody went anywhere though while the snow was so deep. Helen had to call up and tell her boss she couldn't get there because of the roads. She was nervous to call because she might lose her job but I guess the snow kept people in town inside too because he said he could get along without her for now.

I missed school. Before Christmas vacation we had been learning to make slanted ovals on our slates. Once we had the oval just right, we would add a little half wave to the bottom right corner and then we would have a cursive letter A. Students who filled their slates with perfectly shaped ovals got a gold star. It wasn't really too hard to make the smoothest ovals if I went very slowly. I got a lot of gold stars that I showed to Ma who looked but never made any comment. Pa said he would give me a nickel if I got one hundred stars. This was easy money. I also wished I was at school so I could hear more about things like Father Hennepin who was a Catholic priest Miss Jordahl told us about. He came all the way from the Netherlands to find waterfalls which he did. Some of the falls he found were in Minneapolis which is a big city about a hundred miles away. They are called St. Anthony - the falls. They are on the Mississippi River which starts in Minnesota if you didn't know that. St. Anthony was a Catholic too and so were the Bertrands.

While I lived with them, we went to mass at St. Mary's every Sunday. Every Sunday after we could travel the roads that is. It took weeks for the roads to clear enough to go out. That first Sunday morning after the roads were passable Mr.

Bertrand got the wagon ready. No one asked me if I wanted to come along. They just must have figured I did. My own family did not go to church much and before I stayed at the Bertrands' I had never been to mass. Ma's sister Maude sometimes came and took me to church with her family but they went to the Methodist church which was on the other end of town. I always liked the singing there.

St. Mary's was much fancier than the Methodist church. It had two big steeples on either side of the door where we went in and the windows had hundreds of bits of colored glasses that made pictures when you looked at them from a distance. Some of the pictures told stories but I had to wait until later to ask Ruth what they meant. My favorite had mostly blue pieces that looked like a big lake. The blue in the glass was a shade of blue that I had never seen before even on a sunny day. It was like the blue that all other blues came from. The lake had a golden boat on it that might have been a barn but it was floating on the water. It had cows and sheep and some other animals lining up to get in it. I couldn't wait to hear what Ruth had to say about that one.

When we got to our row - way at the front so Oma could see - we had to do a little, short squat. Ruth showed me how to do it before we went in. She told me all the things to watch for which was very helpful. She forgot to tell me about the Latin though. At first I thought the priest was speaking

German as most of the families I recognized in the pews were German. But it didn't sound much like the things Oma said. I was confused and must have looked it because Ruth leaned over to me and whispered, "Latin." I knew about the Romans and all from school but had never heard any of the words. Latin, you know, is a dead language. That means not very many people speak it and those who do don't know how to pronounce it.

At first I thought it was strange to not be able to tell what the priest was saying. But once I got used to it, I liked it. It seemed dignified and creepy at the same time.

After mass was over, the Bertrands took me to my Aunt Rosie's house in town where my parents were staying. I had thought about that visit all week. It was the first time I would see my family since Christmas and the fire. The Bertrands came in to say hello but then they left and I got to stay with everyone and have Sunday dinner. My littlest brother Bunny was already bigger than the last time I saw him and he could stand up and take steps. Ma had to keep after him all the time because now he could really get into mischief. My sisters and I swapped stories about the weeks since we had seen each other. Maudie had been learning how to crochet from our grandmother and Mabel had read eight whole books since we had last been together. She liked to read as much as I did.

At dinner I sat next to Pa. This meant squeezing in between him and my cousin Cecil but Cecil moved over so I could get in. I had to straddle the table leg but I didn't mind that. Pa asked me how I was getting on and I said, "Fine." He said I should remember how lucky I was and I said I did. He tousled my hair like he usually did and then we ate the pork roast, potatoes, rolls and everything that my Aunt Rosie had made. Before it got dark Pa took me back to the Bertrands' place. While I stayed at the Bertrands', Sunday afternoons were the best part of the whole week except that they made me cry even though I tried not to.

On Monday I got up early to do my chores. Some were the same kinds of things I did at home - like filling the wood box and breaking up the ice on the watering troughs - but the Bertands' were dairy farmers so milking had to be done twice each day. The first milking started before dawn and the second was done right before supper. We had had a cow at home. I don't know what had happened to her though since the house burned. She had probably ended up at one of Ma's sisters. Ma usually did the milking. It didn't take her long - maybe fifteen minutes before she had gotten what the cow would give. Sometimes she had one of my sisters do it for her. Mabel was pretty good at milking but my sister Maude didn't seem to care much for it. Ma said my hands were too small.

Milking at the Bertrands' was nothing like at our place. It took hours. There were fifteen cows in the barn and everyone of those cows had to be milked twice a day. Each one took the same fifteen minutes our one took. That's about eight hours a day. Mr. Bertrand couldn't do it all alone. Mrs. Bertrand helped some, and Helen too when she was not at Kuske's Drug Store. But I bet you can guess who was the best milker on the farm. There was something about the way she could fit herself almost totally under the cow that made Oma extremely good at getting the milk. In order to do this, she had to have her own stool. She turned her nose up at the sturdy model her son used. Hers was so short it seemed to me like she could just as well have sat on the floor of the barn. When she sat, she gathered up her skirts and slipped them between her legs until she looked like she was wearing pants. Then she squatted down balancing on her tiny stool and milk away. She whizzed along, one cow after another. I am pretty sure she averaged two cows milked for every one of Mr. Bertrand's but I didn't think my pointing this out would have been welcome information - at least not to him.

No one actually said my hands were too small and, as a matter of fact, I think they might have been close to the same size as Oma's, but I wasn't allowed to milk any of these cows either. There was lots of other work for me to do in the milking barn. The place had to be spic and span Mr. Bertrand said or he couldn't sell his milk. Cows in a barn make a big mess and that mess smells awful until you get used to it which I did after a while. Cleaning up wasn't such a bad job. The barn was dusty but dry. The cows were all held in their stalls by a halter so I didn't have to worry about getting kicked unless I forgot and got too close.

As it turned out I was often in the barn alone with Oma. Until that morning we hadn't interacted much. I did my work and she did hers. Then on this particular day she looked up at me and said, "Fetch me dat."

At first I thought I must have misheard. She didn't speak English. But she made the meaning of the words clear when she both nodded her head and pointed at the empty pail she wanted me to bring. When I finally understood and brought her the pail, she took it, then handed me the one she had been milking into and, with a sly wink, said, "Take dis one."

I had the feeling she had purposely let me in on her secret. Maybe she was grooming me to be her ally. I didn't mind too much. Only I didn't want to get on the wrong side of Mrs. Bertrand who, if there were two camps in the house, was not in the one that Oma was in. I thought it best to go along without over-committing myself. This approach is not difficult for children because all you have to do is pretend you don't really understand what adults are talking about and they are satisfied.

Also I was pretty safe since Mrs. Bertrand spent little time in the barn. She did her share of the milking and then went back to her own world, the house. In that world Oma never spoke a word of English and officially Mrs. Bertrand was the head of the kitchen. She organized the food, decided on the meals and kept anyone in line who crossed into her domain. I never saw Oma openly challenge Mrs. Bertrand but it was becoming clear that she had the heart of a rebel.

Later that same day when I was carrying in the cookstove wood, I noticed Oma adding something that she had pinched between her fingers to the stewpot. Mrs Bertrand had her back turned and Oma looked at me with a short, fat finger to her lips and then gave me another of her winks. "Zaubertrank," she whispered. Mrs. Bertrand turned at the sound but she only rolled her eyes, her standard response to Oma, and went back to work on the biscuit dough. She didn't like to give any weight whatsoever to Oma's mutterings and seemed to take it as a moral offense that her mother-in-law failed to speak English.

For myself, I felt the need to know what sober trunk was given that I was going to be eating a bowl of that stew in the next little while. "Poison" appealed to my sense of drama but why Oma would want to poison the whole family I couldn't guess. Mrs. Bertrand maybe but she seemed to like the rest of us. I was after all her newly recruited accomplice. Also if she planned to wipe us all out in a single stroke would she tell me in advance? Maybe it was a warning so I could escape? I couldn't very well ask her with Mrs. Bertrand standing right there so I ran back to the wood pile and found the flattest piece of wood in the stack. Next I went to the coal bin and picked out a pointy piece. Working as carefully as I could and being a gold-star cursive letter-maker, I sounded out and then wrote out what I thought I had heard Oma whisper, SOBER TRUNK. I wrote it all in capitals as we had not mastered our small letters yet. For good measure, I added a question mark but it was fatter than I liked and so looked more like an explanation point. It was the best I could do. I filled my arms with stove wood, turned over the one I had written on and set it on top. By the time I got back to the kitchen Oma was gone and Mrs. Bertrand was just about to sample the stew.

"No!" I yelped.

She dropped the long spoon with a clatter.

"Too hot," was all I could think to say. "You might burn your tongue." Weak, very weak I knew. I wanted to disappear and for a moment I thought that from Mrs. Bertrand's startled expression she might want me to disappear as well. But then she cocked her head to one side and smiled. Her smile reminded me of Ruth's.

"Why you sweet boy! What a thoughtful boy to care if I hurt myself."

I was afraid she was going to hug me. Adults are so strange. But she just patted me on the shoulder and said, "You go put the wood down and then get ready for dinner." She kept smiling and seemed to forget she was going to taste the stew. Instead she pulled the biscuits from the oven and got a basket ready to put them in. Just then, Oma came in from outside. While she was getting out of the heavy gray cape she always wore to the barn and back, Mrs. Bertrand still smiling walked into the pantry. I had seconds to act. I pulled the piece of wood I had written on and rushed over to Oma. She looked down at it in complete bewilderment. Oh no, of course, she couldn't read. Why had I not thought of that? My own grandmother could barely read and none of her siblings could at all. Now, I was doomed to die of poison stew. It had been a good life, except for our house burning down, but way too short. There was a lot I still wanted to do. I thought I might make a good hockey player or quarterback on the football team. I had not yet seen a motion picture show or ridden on a train. I had been planning to read all of Jack London's books. Now it was all over. I wondered if it hurt to eat poison.

But Oma was still holding the piece of wood and continuing to stare at it. Her face seemed to contort with the effort to make sense of it but then I realized she was laughing. Not just a tiny chuckle but a throw your head back and shake kind of laugh. She could read after all. Oma was a woman of unexpected talents.

"Es ist gut," she whispered into my ear once she had regained control.

"Gut," she repeated. "Es ist Magie, little Philip. Es ist gut." Thankfully, Oma was not a hugger but she reached out and cradled my chin in her hand. She laughed again but not so extremely this time.

"Es ist gut."

I could make out good. Gut is good. Sober trunk is good. Maybe tasty good? Maybe I had made all this fuss over a spice. But magie? I wanted to just ask her, What does magie mean? But Mrs. Bertrand was coming back in from the pantry and her smile had disappeared.

"Tell everyone dinner is ready, Phil."

"Oma, you can serve up the stew." Mrs. Bertrand always spoke English to Oma but she spoke really slowly and used gestures as well - just in case. She held up a bowl at Oma's eye level and pretended to dip the ladle into the hot stew.

"Time to eat."

I had no choice but to leave the room. The rest of the household was scattered. Mary was in the attic. Mr. Bertrand was in the barn. Helen was at the sewing machine and the little boys were crawling around underneath. Helen would scoop them up on her way to the table. I kept rolling magie over in my mind as I went from room to room and house to barn. Magie? It sounded a lot like the name of the Wise Men that come to bring gifts to the baby Jesus. I couldn't exactly remember what the gifts were. One was something that smelled good maybe? Yes, and now I was back to spices. But magie or something like it was the name of the people not the gifts. Who were they? Miss Jordahl had shown us a brightly colored picture of them before Christmas. They had the most amazing outfits. Like kings of far-away lands or....sorcerers. They followed a bright star all the way to the stable. I had meant to look for that star on Christmas Eve but I forgot.

Mr. Bertrand said he would come in a minute. This would not make Mrs. Bertrand happy. She believed that people should be seated at the table immediately after she had had the thought that they should be seated at the table. I walked back slowly so as to delay bringing her the news. When I got back everyone else was gathered around the table. Lars and Leo were in matching high chairs. Mary was seated next to Leo and Helen was between him and Lars. Oma had finished ladling stew but had not sat down. There was always a contest between her and Mrs. Bertrand over who would sit down last. The winner was the one still standing, and Oma was hard to beat. She would often fake sit and then pop back up. Like magic! That must be it. Sober trunk was magic. Oma had seasoned the stew with an enchanted herb - magie. I remembered then that Oma was well-known for foraging in the woods for strange plants and mushrooms. Even Ma had talked about her wandering about in the countryside. Her remarks did not lack admiration as Ma herself was an expert forager. She knew all kinds of Native recipes for cure-alls and such. But Ma didn't have any truck with magic. My ma's view of the world was in every way unmagical - if you know what I mean.

Mr. Bertrand came in just in time. It was plain that Mrs. Bertrand was about to blow a gasket with the stew sitting there in bowls getting cooled off and the twins starting to fuss and Oma refusing to sit down. He washed up at the sink and then sat down oblivious to the enchantment about to come his way. I could not wait. He was always the one to say grace. We all folded our hands and bowed our heads. I looked through my eyelashes so I could see who sat last. Both Oma and Mrs. Bertrand were in their chairs but sure enough Mr. Bertrand had barely finished the 'nnn' in amen when Oma was up again.

"Honig," she said, for the biscuits - honey.

I have to admit I was disappointed. The stew tasted just like stew. Tasty but not as good as ma's or my grandmother's. I had no idea what sort of magic was supposed to happen but I didn't feel anything unusual at all. I didn't expect visions or anything like that. Though they might have been interesting but I did figure there would be tingling of some kind. Tingling and maybe a whirling sensation. Nothing. There was just ordinary fullness and sleepiness which was probably due to the four biscuits I ate - with honig. I did my best to watch everyone else closely to see if they showed any signs of being under a spell. The twins were demanding to get down and Helen was helping them. They always wanted to get out of their chairs as soon as they could after a meal and Helen was normally in charge.

Mr. Bertrand seemed relaxed and happy but he generally was after dinner. Pretty soon he would light his pipe. Just like Pa, he always had a pipe after dinner. Oma was scurrying around no faster or slower than usual. Mrs. Bertrand announced that she had to go check on something or other. On her way out of the room, she told Helen to clean up from dinner. That left Mary. Mary was a sickly girl who mostly seemed sad. I would be sad too if I could not go to school, could not go outside and could not see my friends. I wouldn't mind the never having to do chores, but I think Mary did mind. Her whole world centered around that table, the attic bedroom and the space in between. So I gave her a good hard look. We were the only ones still at the table. And what do you think? I thought I did see something in her face that wasn't usually there. A sort of brightness, maybe a sparkle in her eyes and even a little pinkness in her cheeks. Normally she had a washed-out look that went with her straggly hair and hunched over shoulders. Now she was sitting up straight and looking alive. She even looked kind of pretty. She pushed back her chair and said to her sister, "Why don't I take the twins while you do the dishes?" That was a first. Helen didn't seem to know what to say. She looked out of the door maybe to see if her ma might come back and tell her what to do but there was no one around to come to her rescue. Even Oma had disappeared.

"All right. Remember they are heavy though. Be careful."

Mary smiled, scooped up the bigger of the twins and planted a giant kiss on his right cheek, "I'll remember."

Magic? I don't know what else it could have been.

Chapter Six: Beautiful Dreamer

After months of being apart, our family finally got back together. We didn't go back to the farm. Just as the big war in Europe was ending, we moved into a house in town. As far as I could tell the town hadn't changed much during the war. For the most part, life had gone as usual. There were some men who had gone to fight. They volunteered or were drafted. The National Guard unit was sent to join the regular army in France. Uncle Ted had gone with that unit and so a distant war had come a little bit closer.

There was a parade downtown when the unit left. Pa was the only one there but I heard him tell Ma, "Henry Bertrand and I were standing there watching the parade when Scully walked by muttering 'dirty kraut.' I thought I might give him a piece of my mind but Henry stopped me. Better not to make a scene but what an old fool that Scully is!"

Pa had been steaming but Ma had just nodded. In some towns having a German name meant you were the enemy but in Sleepy Eye there were so many people with German names. They were business owners, farmers, teachers, neighbors. None of them seemed much like an enemy to me. Some of the old folks still spoke German - like Oma - but the younger ones hardly knew a word of German and didn't seem to care much if they did. In school, they said the Pledge of Allegiance just like everybody else. I hardly knew Mr. Scully but I sort of wished that he had gotten a piece of Pa's mind. I would never forget the time I spent with the Bertrands and the way they treated me like part of their family. I also would never forget all the German swear words l learned from listening to Oma. They would come in handy later.

People where we lived had been sure the war would be over in no time once the Yanks got involved. There was a lot of pride in those who had gone overseas. Most homes displayed flags and at the train depot there were posters of Uncle Sam and Lady Liberty. Naturally, people worried about whether their brothers, sons or husbands would come home. It was a big relief that fall when soldiers started to come back. There was another much bigger parade and a concert at the bandstand. This time we all walked over to watch the parade and listen to the music. It was a mild day for November and the sun was out. Hundreds of people lined both sides of Main Street on either side of Third Avenue. It was hard to even find a place to stand. Except for Bunny, we kids got to roam freely while Pa and Ma found a place at the curb. We made our way through the crowd stopping now and then to watch the marching band or the Clydesdale horses. I liked best the big bass drum.

"Boom! Boom! Boom!" You could yell as loud as you wanted while the drummer was walking by. So I did.

This parade didn't have any people walking on stilts or clowns throwing candy though. It was a more serious kind of parade because of the soldiers. They didn't all come home. Mr. Miller who had played the banjo at our house the Thanksgiving before had lost a son in the war. His name was Ruben; he had been the middle of five brothers and he had died in a trench in northeastern France. Mr. Scully's son had not died but he had to stay in the hospital for a long time while his burns healed. And there were others too. It didn't make much sense to me - going so far away just to get shot or burned or something.

We didn't find our parents again until people started gathering around the bandstand. Mabel had made Clay take her hand in the crowd and Maude had made Chilly take hers. Chilly said he didn't see why if I could walk around by myself that he couldn't but Maude made him anyway. I wouldn't have wanted to hold my sister's hand either. Embarrassing.

I stood next to Pa while the music played. It wasn't dancing type music like Uncle Vernon had played but some of it was it was pretty rousing. I was hoping it might help people be less sad about the men who weren't coming back.

Standing on the other side of Pa was Wally Berg's pa. Wally Berg was one of the first boys I had made friends with when I moved to town. I didn't know Pa even knew his pa but Pa knew a lot of people.

When the band took a break I could hear Mr. Berg saying to Pa, "There's been a dozen cases right here in the county. Some have died of it."

"Is that so? How's it spreading I wonder."

"Who knows?! It started in Spain and now it's going around like wild fire."

"That don't seem right! How come everybody isn't talking about it."

"I guess they don't want to scare people and then the papers are so full of the war. But don't you worry it's happening right here in Sleepy Eye."

"Poor fellas."

Pa didn't farm after we moved to town except for the occasional help he gave my uncles and grandfather. He did continue to haul milk and cream as he had done for nearly a decade. He told me once that he partly liked the job because it was steady and partly because it gave him the chance to talk to farmers. I think maybe that Pa's friendly face and easy way was a welcome break from the farmer's long work day. Farming can be a lonesome occupation. Most looked forward to news that came from the world outside their own 'back forty.' My pa picked up cream and delivered the news. After all, he had been from one end of the county to the other.

"Did you hear? Art Bekke bought the Lloyd place."

"No!"

"He did. Bought the whole place."

"He did?"

"Yup."

"I thought he was looking at some land over southeast there."

"I don't know what happened to that. I guess he figured he could get a better price for the Lloyd place. They wanted to sell that place pretty bad since Bertram died."

"The boy didn't want to farm it?"

"Not those boys."

"I suppose not."

"Bert, Jr. might have but he's got his hands full now down at the mill."

"I guess so. How many more are there?"

"Just three. Four boys. There's a girl too."

"She moved to the Cities, didn't she?"

"She did. Married some fellow that works in a factory there. Not a farmer."

"People do that I guess. Art should do pretty well with that land."

"Yes sir. He knows what he's doing. That's for sure. He'll get it under the plow in no time."

"Yup."

Pa said that a man could feel adrift, cut-off without news about his neighbor, without knowing how things are. A farmer's wife often had more contact with the outside world. She might have a church group or a get-together for quilting or canning. She learned plenty of news and she might share some with her husband but it was still good for a man to hear some on his own. At least it seemed that way to the farmers that Pa picked up milk from. They trusted him with their milk and with their stories. He was a person who did not carry either lightly.

In the early years, Pa had used a horse-drawn wagon to go from farm to farm. But later he got a motorized truck. It had a flatbed in the back with wide slats to make an enclosure that kept the milk cans in. In the front was a passenger cab that was open on each side but had a roof to keep off the rain and snow. Pa's was not the first motorized truck in the county. There were plenty of others. But his was one of the first with air-filled tires. None of our neighbors had seen such a thing. They were convinced that it was a crazy idea and they weren't afraid to say so.

"Oren, you better not take that thing down the road to Bekke's. Those big rocks'll pop those tires for sure. What are you gonna do with all the milk then? Sit by the side of the road and wait for help?"

"Been to Bekke's this morning. Nothing popped. Maybe not so bad as you remember it." This Pa said with a smile as he thought it was best to smile when you are proving that a person is mistaken.

That farmer might have been impressed with the durability of the new fangled tires but he did not let on and merely replied with a "harrumph" as if to say, "That's one road, one time. I'll wait and see."

Since I was the oldest boy, sometimes I would get to go with Pa on his rounds. I loved to do so for lots of reasons. For one thing it was something different to do. I could sit up in the cab and look out at the countryside which seemed to fly by as we traveled from farm to farm. The world I saw from the seat of Pa's truck was something new and exciting -

Page 123

even if I had seen it before by foot or in a horse drawn wagon. It was transformed by way of a unique vantage point.

Pa and I talked very little on these trips. The roar of the engine and the thrum of the tires on packed dirt made conversation impossible. But the trip itself provided all the interest a boy could hope for.

Another reason was that it meant I had been chosen. Pa had wanted me along. He must have thought I was good company. It wasn't really that I thought anyone else might be asked to go instead. For some reason, the girls had little interest in the truck or the trek. They seemed to prefer to stay at home with Ma. The other boys were too little. Or one couldn't go without the other. At any rate, I had the status of the oldest son and so I was chosen.

One more reason I liked to go with Pa was that I liked to see the way people acted when they were around him. I could tell that people were happy when they saw Pa's truck pull up to their barn. They waved and smiled. Then they took their time in their conversations as if they were not ready for Pa to leave. Pa was always friendly. He asked each farmer about his family, his crops, his animals. He commiserated with them about their problems and showed genuine pleasure in their accomplishments. He was neither hurried nor slow in his business. He always seemed to understand when it was the right time to conclude, to get back in the truck and drive away. I often looked back at the farmers as we pulled away. Most had a smile and that made me proud.

Back in town, I helped Pa with errands- picking up a new pitchfork, buying a bag of sugar for Ma, or taking a milk can in to be repaired. When errands and rounds were done, Pa might decide to stop in at the saloon. This was a highlight of the trip. Going from bright sunlight into the smoky darkness of the interior felt a little like I was stepping into a dream. When Pa ordered his own drink he got a cider for me. Cool and sweet, it was so refreshing that I took my time sipping. Normally I was in a rush to eat or drink. Ma would say 'you'd think someone was going to come and take the food away.' But in the dark saloon with Pa, I wanted the coolness and the haziness of the dream to last.

Once school started in the fall there were fewer opportunities for me to join Pa on his rounds. The days grew shorter and it got colder. Snow fell and made great waves along the fence rows. The stove had to be well-banked before bedtime or the house would get so cold I could see my own breath even inside. It was during those dark days of winter that Pa got sick. At first, it seemed like any bad cold. His head ached and his throat was sore. He coughed and coughed. Ma made some cough syrup with honey and whiskey which normally did the trick but Pa kept right on coughing. His fever got so bad it made him shake and he was so tired he couldn't get into his truck and go out on his rounds.

He didn't have any choice but to go to the doctor. Dr. Bauer looked down his throat and listened to his chest. He told Pa to take some aspirin and get as much rest as he could. Pa came home, took the aspirin and went to bed. A few hours later his fever finally broke and he could sleep. He slept through one night and into the next. When he woke before dawn, he felt better. He was coughing still but he said his head didn't ache so bad.

When she saw him putting his overalls on, Ma said, "Why don't you stay home one more day and get a good rest like the doctor said?"

"Who's gonna pick up the milk and cream? I've got farmers counting on me. And anyway I ain't so dog-tired that I can't drive that truck around." He went back to work.

Dr. Bauer had been treating lots of others who had symptoms like Pa's. Some were getting better like he seemed to be. Some got worse. And it spread so quickly from one person to the next. At school we had to wear masks and some adults wore them too but still the hospital in New Ulm was full. It wasn't just babies and old people - many were just like Pa - young and strong.

Life at home settled back to normal after the hushed hours of Pa's sickness. Work, school, chores, meal times filled

Page 126

the short days just as they always had. Finally those days began to grow longer again and the snow receded. As it melted, it mingled with the earth and the world became gray. Even the sky turned gray. The brisk, crystal-clear mornings of winter were gone. Overhead the clouds blocked the sun and on the ground muddy slush seeped through my boots and up my pant legs.

Pa seemed to be getting stronger but still tired easily. I never heard him complain but we all noticed that he was quieter than he used to be. He would forget to tousle my hair when he walked by and didn't raise Bunny up over his head like usual. He didn't tease the girls and he didn't tell Ma the food was 'sure good.' He moved through the day as if that was the most he could do. And then he started to cough again. It wasn't much of a cough at first and he didn't seem nearly so sick as he had before. But then all of a sudden it got worse, much worse.

Pa couldn't seem to get his breath and when he coughed there was blood. We went to bed that night to the sound of Pa's dry wheezing and his desperate attempts to breathe. I couldn't bear to hear it so I covered my head with my pillow until I finally fell asleep. At some point in the night, Ma realized she couldn't do anything more for Pa at home. He would have to go to the hospital. She didn't drive and we still had no phone.

She shook me awake and said, "You've got to go over to Gilles's and call the doctor." This was part of being the oldest boy that wasn't so great. Ma needed the girls close by to help her and the other boys were too little. I would never have let them go anyway. I dragged myself out of bed.

"Pa's bad. He has to go to the hospital. You need to go to Gilles's and call,' Ma said again as if she understood the need for me to move had not sunk in. Still half-asleep, I shoved my feet into my shoes and pulled on the coat Ma was holding out for me. I couldn't tell what time it was except I knew it had to be long before dawn. Outside the sky was moonless and the spring air was damp. No light from any window led the way. All I had to do was walk down our walk and cross the street but I got turned around and stumbled off in the wrong direction. The blankness around me seemed so alien and strange. When I came to the outline of a big oak tree I knew I was not on the way to the Gilles's. I blinked back tears, took a deep breath and started back in the other direction.

Like most everyone else in town the Gilleses were still asleep. The house was dark and quiet. There was no dog to rouse the family. I knocked as loudly as I could. I thought the whole world must have heard for all the noise I was making. I even yelled out, "Mr. Gilles! I need to use your phone."

What if nobody came and while I stood there Pa coughed himself to death? I tried again - this time kicking the door to make it rattle. Finally, lights appeared above me and then, at last, someone was at the door. It was Mrs. Gilles. I told her my story as clear and even as I could but my voice sounded echoey - like someone else was talking. Then my legs gave out and someone caught me in their arms. I was laid out on the sofa and the adults took over - calling the hospital, finding jackets and gloves, lighting lanterns. Mr. Gilles walked out the door with a lantern while Mrs. Gilles bustled around the house like someone who knows just what to do in an emergency.

I lay alone for a while on the sofa in the Gilles's front room. I felt clammy and the winter jacket I still had on was heavy. Mrs. Gilles seemed to have forgotten about me so I got up off the sofa and walked back into the night. It was still dark but high above I could just make out the faint glow of the moon behind fast-moving clouds.

Standing on the side of the street, I watched as the ambulance pulled up in front of our house. It hadn't sounded its siren. I suppose there were no vehicles on the road to warn. The front light was on at our house. It threw a pale beam out onto the front yard. Three men stepped out of the ambulance and then reappeared inside the beam. Ma came out for a minute and talked to them but I was too far away to hear what they said. Two of the men walked back to the ambulance and the third went into the house. The two men came back with a long white stretcher and they followed Ma into the house. Standing just to the right of our front door was Mr. Gilles still holding his lantern. It seemed like forever before anything else happened. Neither Mr. Gilles or I moved from our spots. Finally, I saw the looming form of the biggest man as he walked backwards out of our front door. Then came the stretcher with Pa lying so still. Then the two other men carrying the other end of the stretcher. Mr. Gilles stepped forward as if to help but the big man waved him away. Then they put Pa in the back of the ambulance and drove away.

Mrs. Gilles came to our house to look after the six of us while Mr. Gilles drove Ma to the hospital in New Ulm. Mrs. Gilles made coffee and fixed breakfast as if it was any morning. She had us wash our faces before we ate and then we all sat at the table and looked at our food. The clock ticked and Mrs. Gilles's skirts swooshed against the kitchen chairs as she walked Bunny up and down. Time seemed to come to a stop but not in a good way. It was like it was stuck. I felt like I was still half asleep or just waking up the way I sometimes did and was still dreaming and the dream kept pulling me back. I couldn't decide whether I wanted to hold onto the dream or whether the dream was a nightmare that I wanted to let go of. My brothers and my sisters and I sat around the table for I don't know how long. Finally it was light and sunlight fell on the table. The little boys grew restless and Clayton started to cry. Mrs. Gilles told him to hush but he wouldn't stop and so she told us we could all leave the table and she cleared the uneaten food away.

I went out behind the house where there was a small shed. I pulled open the door and sat down. From inside I could see the weak sunshine falling in through the gaps between the slats. It made faint yellow lines on the floor of the shed and above these I could see dust dance in the strips of light. The shed was cold and the floor was damp. I had not thought to bring my coat out with me but I didn't want to go back to the house to get it. I sat and watched the dust dance and tried not to see the image of Pa on the stretcher in my mind. Even small boys sometimes think about death. They know when animals die. Like our old black dog who couldn't get up anymore. Or like the little kitten my younger brother, Clayton had held in his two small hands for most of an hour trying to get it warm again. Little boys know about people dying too. When one of Ma's aunts died my parents went to the funeral and took Mabel with them. I guess because she was the oldest. I had half-wanted to go too because I had never seen a dead person before. I thought some then about what deadness would look like. Ma said after the funeral that her aunt had looked at peace but I didn't find that that description helped much. Did at peace mean she looked happy or just that she wasn't moving? Even though little boys think about death, they never imagine it coming really close.

Maudie poked her head in the shed, "Aunt Ellie is here and she's got dinner on. Come on in." I didn't think I was hungry but I followed her into the house anyway. Our kitchen was filled with women. Mrs. Gilles was gone but my mother's sisters were there and so was my grandmother. The cookstove was hot and the smell of roasting meat filled the room. Coffee was on and all the women were doing something. Aunt Pearl had Bunny. She was so small that they were nearly the same size. Aunt Ellie was pulling the roast from the oven. Aunt Maude was setting the table and my grandmother was cutting thick slices of bread.

Everyone was talking to someone. Aunt Pearl was talking to Bunny, telling him he was such a pretty boy. Aunt Maude was talking to her mother, telling her that was enough bread unless there were going to be men and there weren't. My grandmother was talking to herself. I couldn't quite hear what she was saying. Aunt Ellie was talking to all the children, telling them to wash up and sit down.

"All right! Sit down. Clay, dry your hands!"

"Wilbur, put that down and come to the table!"

"Phil, wash up now. You don't want dinner to get cold."

"Here Mabel, you watch the baby for a minute."

"That's right Maudie help yourself."

None of the women sat down. They hovered around us, giving constant instructions about the size of the portion, the heat of the stewed tomatoes, the blade of the sharp knife.

We ate. I was surprised and a little ashamed to find that the food tasted good. We ate slowly to make the meal last as long as we could - not sure of what would follow. Finally, when we couldn't eat another bite, we pushed our plates away. While the women cleaned up, they called out more instructions. They had things for us to do if we couldn't think of any ourselves. Mostly these were the household chores that Pa and Ma would have had us do but they added some extra things as well. Our parents' bed was still unmade in the middle of the day. The girls could have made it but instead Aunt Ellie told them to gather up the sheets for washing. It was not washing day so that seemed strange but the aunts were in charge and the girls did what they were told. The floors needed to be swept and rugs shaken. Chilly, Clayton and I were sent out to bring in wood for the stove and to clean up the woodshed. It almost seemed like company was coming the way our aunts were hurrying around cleaning and straightening.

I was grateful for a task and the chance to go back outside. Clay was not much help. Chilly and I did most of the work but we were careful to hand our little brother a piece of wood now and then so that he didn't go running back in the house and get in the way. Even during a dark time, we were still boys and sooner or later had to start throwing wood instead of stacking it. The pieces were small at first but they began to grow in size. Our energy in launching them grew as well. Any grownup watching would have been certain one of us would lose an eye. This always seemed an empty threat to me as I did not know a single child who had lost an eye from any sort of projectile being hurled but, given the frequency of the adult warning, there should have been no child left on earth without a missing eye. We did, of course, go too far. Like any other boys we found it impossible to stop until we had gone too far. Chilly and I both had good aim and hurled our specially selected pieces of wood just close enough and hard enough to sting but not to leave a welt. Little Clay, however, was not so expert and kept running between us to try and be part of the game. We were either ignoring him or yelling at him to get out of the way and, inevitably, he caught one of the wood projectiles on the side of the head. It hit pretty hard because he had been running too close to Chilly just as he had let it fly. In fact, it knocked him to the ground. He lay there for a moment holding his head and curling up in a ball. For a second, I was afraid we had knocked him unconscious - but then he started to scream. Oh boy, that was the loudest scream I'd ever heard. He just kept screaming - and crying - and kicking. We tried to calm him down and see if he was hurt but he kicked us when we got close and kept right on screaming.

Naturally one of our aunts came out of the house to see what all the noise was about. It was Aunt Maude. Our aunts came in four sizes. Aunt Pearl was tiny in every way. She and our ma looked most alike. Aunt Rosie was skinny but tall - at least tall compared to the rest. Ellie was short and round. Aunt Maude was big in both directions. Both her stature and personality could be intimidating. She eyed Chilly and me like we were little insects she was just about to flatten with her broom. She picked Clayton up, brushed him off and pulled his hand away from his forehead so she could assess the damage. He was no longer screaming. He was whimpering and sniffling. There was no blood - lucky for us - but you could see a bright red spot that had already started to grow.

Aunt Maude enveloped Clay in her arms and said, "Let's go in and put a cool cloth on that bump. You'll be all right."

He made a small smile - his eyes stilled brimmed with tears. She turned to us. On a normal day we would have received a severe scolding and maybe more, but Aunt Maude just looked at us and sighed. Deflated and wordless we cleaned up our mess. We filled our arms with stacks of wood and went into the house. It was warm and dry and practically shone with all the cleaning and straightening. The work was done and there was nothing left to do. There was an empty silence where all the familiar activity had been. It was like we and the house were taking a long, deep breath. Our aunts and grandmother sat down around the table and we children sat ourselves down either in their laps or on a chair close by. No one spoke and we all struggled for a place to look.

After long minutes had passed, Aunt Ellie, who had the best voice in the family, started to sing "Beautiful Dreamer." She began softly almost to herself. Aunt Pearl joined her and then the rest of the women started to sing. The older of us who knew the words sang along. The little ones did a sort of humming-singing so as not to be left out. There was a short pause after the song ended and then Mabel started us on "In the Good Old Summertime." When that was over, Chilly asked if we could sing "Row, Row Your Boat." One song followed another. There was no talking just the singing.

Ma came home just before dark. She stepped into the parlor and her sisters went to her. We children stayed in the kitchen but I could still hear when Ma said, "He's gone."

In one way, I knew what that meant because children know about death. My pa had died. In a bigger way though, I could not really fathom what that meant. My life from now on would have no Pa in it. Our family had no father. My mother had no husband. The world had no Oren McCoy. The terrible thought that was unthinkable just kept opening up into larger and larger empty spaces. I would not be able to keep myself from slipping over the edge into the hole made by the death of my father. It was a deep, deep hole of sadness.

I can't tell you any more about the day my pa died. We might have kept singing. I don't remember.

Chapter Seven: Red Rover

There was a funeral for Pa at the Methodist church. People sent flowers and brought food over. For the first few weeks our house was always overflowing with relatives, friends and even with people we hardly knew. Nothing about that time was normal and the most ordinary things seemed distant and strange. We had not lived in the house long and much of that time had been interrupted by Pa's sickness. It was hard to get an anchor in the sea of unfamiliarity. Even the school year went by with my hardly knowing it. When summer came it seemed odd that the sun was shining when the world still seemed so dark. But our lives had to go on and we had to fend for ourselves without Pa there to take care of things.

A widow with six kids, Ma didn't have too many choices. But she was already an expert at making a little go a long way. We always had food on the table. She kept a kitchen garden behind our house in town just as she had on the farm. The end of the war led to some surpluses and one thing that there was plenty of was rice. Ma bought it by the twenty-pound bagful. I have to admit I got pretty tired of eating rice. I could live without ever seeing rice pudding again. While grain was cheap, meat was much harder to come by. When the larder got so low that there was nothing to flavor the stew with, Ma sent me to the butcher's. I was supposed to ask him for a bone for our dog. I hated doing it. I knew that the butcher knew that we didn't have any old dog. He never let on though. He just wrapped the bone up and handed it to me.

In a small town like ours, there was no work for an uneducated woman of thirty-six outside the home. So Ma did what she knew how to do. She did laundry - other people's. Since we didn't own a washing machine, Ma did it all by hand.

On the first Monday after school let out for the summer, she put me to work. I helped carry the large laundry tubs up from the cellar to the backyard. I think Ma must have looked forward to doing the laundry in the fresh air after spending the cold months doing it all in the dank, unheated cellar. One tub had to have boiling water in it. I was the one who brought the full, hot kettles from the kitchen to the tub. Ma kept calling out, "Be careful! Don't trip. Don't splash any of that water out."

I sure didn't want to get scalded so I was extra careful. The actual washing was done on a scrub board. Fortunately nobody expected me to do that. That was the part my two sisters helped Ma with. First, they dissolved lye shavings in the steaming water. Then each sheet and pillowcase had to be scrubbed up and down with the hot, soapy water. By the time the day was over, their hands were beet red and raw.

Whites went in the hot water first so that they didn't come out drab and gray. But the soapy water was precious and Ma was stingy with it. She used it over and over again. Work clothes went in last. A separate tub was used for the rinsing. It didn't have to be hot so I just filled it from the outside spigot. After the bedding and clothes had been through both the washing and rinsing tubs, it was wrung out and hung up to dry. In the winter the things froze stiff on the line and had to be shaken in order to soften up. But now that the days were warmer, a gentle breeze made them soft and dry. We all helped pull the laundry off the line. I don't suppose there is any better smell in the world than that of a sheet that has dried in the sun. I smooshed my face in each one and took a deep breath.

The last thing was for Ma to fold it all into stacks. Then that washing day was over. The ironing would take her another day.

Even in a small town like ours there were women who thought they had better things to do than spend the day doing laundry. It started with just one neighbor but soon enough, a number of women who could afford to pay someone else to do it were bringing their laundry to Ma. Some of them probably even had wringer washers in their own homes but they thought that the new machines didn't get things nearly white enough and that Ma's old-fashioned methods got better results. Ma never said what she thought about doing other people's laundry. Our family needed the money.

Of course, there was never any extra. If a boy wanted to go to a picture - I couldn't wait to see "The Garage" with Fatty Arbuckle - he would have to get the cash himself. I got a job delivering papers. There was the local paper, *The Sleepy Eye Progressive* which just about everyone in town subscribed to. There were also the Cities' papers. Most people wanted either the *Minnesota Daily Star* which came in the evening or the morning paper *The Minneapolis Tribune* or both. Some

wanted the St. Paul paper the *Pioneer Press.* There was not a
family in town who didn't get one kind of paper or another.

The morning edition had to go out before it was even
light. I got up in the still, summer darkness and walked down
to the post office where I waited for the big truck to pull in.
The driver's name was Boise Hopkins. I guess he was from
Boise, Idaho unless his parents had actually named him Boise
to begin with. He never said. He hardly spoke a word. Me
and the other boys who delivered the papers were already
there when Boise drove up. He would get pretty hot under
the collar if we weren't right at the spot when he was ready to
unload. Like always he had a cigarette stuck in his teeth. I
never saw him once without one. He had the cigarette, hand-
rolled, in his mouth and a cap pulled down low on his
forehead when he jumped down from the cab. He opened up
the back of the truck which was about two-thirds full. The
other third had been dropped off at towns before ours. He
jumped up inside and threw the bundles out one at a time to
each of us. Once we had our papers we were supposed to get
out of the way. There was no chit-chat either with Boise or
among us boys while the papers were being passed out.

Boise did not wait around while we organized our
bundles. He was back in the truck, door slammed shut and in
gear before you could say, "Jack Robinson." He gave us boys
a quick wave and then he was off to the next town. I never

did learn one thing about him in all the years he brought the papers except that he was always on time and that he didn't like to wait around.

Once he was on his way, the chatter started up among us boys. We said a thing or two about Boise in a teasing-complaining sort of way - things we would never say to his face.

"It wouldn't kill him to say 'Good Morning.'"

"The cat must have got his tongue!"

Wally Berg called him 'Bashful Boise' which made the rest of us laugh every single time we heard it. After the jibes at Boise were finished we exchanged some news like how Al Scobe had tied a toy caboose to his cat's tail and watched her drag it around his yard yesterday afternoon. Or we might swap some lies. Carl Christiansen told us about how he had set fire to his sister's doll house. It had crackled like anything, said Carl, and had spit sparks thirty feet in the air before he had pretended he was a fireman and put it out with the garden hose. I didn't believe a word of that story. For one thing, Carl was alive telling it and if it had been true, his pa would have killed him on the spot. But Carl was a pretty good story-teller so I didn't say his story was full of holes even though it was. There was no point in ruining a half-way decent story with minor objections like no basis in reality. We boys might also talk about some picture we had seen as we all loved to see the pictures. After Carl finished the no-doubt-made-up doll house fire story, Al told us about "The Mask of Zorro" which had just been to town and to which he had been with his older brother. Man, did that show sounded exciting. That Douglas Fairbanks sure knew how to thrash his sword around. There was one thing we never talked about and that was our families - or any subject of that sort. This fact always confounded my ma who later in the day would ask me a question like "How is Mrs. Berg's broken wrist healing?" "How would I know?" I would say with disgust. Then she would just shake her head as if to say boys certainly are a mystery.

Naturally, we didn't just stand there on the street corner talking all day. People wanted their papers. Some silent signal would tell us it was time to go and off we would drift away with our papers. Like most newspaper boys in town, Wally and Carl did their deliveries on bikes. Our family didn't own a bike so I did my route on foot dragging an old wagon behind me. You might think this was a disadvantage but I walked fast and without a bike I could get right up next to the house. I didn't have to slow down and my toss was pretty accurate. Very few papers ended up in the bushes.

When I got to the first stop, it was still dark but lights inside homes had started coming on here and there. The first sounds of the day were breaking through the quiet of the night. People were getting up. Coffee was brewing. Bedclothes were being shaken out and men were at the sink shaving. Dogs were barking. Everybody expected that the paper would be there when they first opened the front door. No one wanted to wait. It was no good their knowing they were at the far end of the route. They didn't want to think about the route or where they were on it. They wanted their paper first thing in the morning. It was part of their morning. They wanted to see who had won the World Series, find out how the peace process was going, learn if women had got the vote, get the latest grain prices. The town paper would also give them the prices on local goods, let them know what was playing at the picture show, tell them when the Elks were meeting and, of course, list the obituaries.

Only months before my pa's obituary had been in the *Sleepy Eye Herald-Dispatch*, "Death Angel is Still Very Active" the title read. It said that Pa was "...well known and liked by all." The words made me proud and sorry at the same time. In a way it seemed that he had already been gone a long time but it was still strange to think that he would not come back. I was trying to get used to the idea that I was a boy with a dead father. I was not a boy without a father, that was not true but my father was dead. He always would be.

As I let go of the last of my papers on the Havemeier's front porch - Mr. Havemeier was standing at his door looking out into the new day, not smiling - I heard the 7:05 east bound freight train pull into town. It gave a long, deep call to announce its arrival. That call could be heard all the way across town. The sound of trains arriving and departing punctuated daily life in our town. It created a rhythm for the days and nights. Already carrying coal and timber from the west, this train would take on wheat at the railroad elevator which stood watch next to the station. It then would carry its load farther east into New Ulm and then north and east into the Cities or south and east all the way to Chicago. It was exciting for a young boy to hear the sound of a train whistle - no matter how often. It was a reminder that in some way I was connected to a bigger world beyond my own small town. If I was in sight of the engineer, I would give him a wave. If he saw me and was in the mood he waved back or better still blew the whistle. What a sweet, transporting sound. It was a call to adventure, an invitation to explore the world outside the wheat and corn fields of my youth. I would answer that call in less than a decade. Then I would seek my fortune in towns and cities far from my own. But for now I was still a boy waving at the engineer from the banks along the rails which ran east and west out of town.

Once my delivery bags were empty, I headed home for my breakfast. Now that the summer sun was out the air had already started to become heavy with heat. I had never noticed before that summer how much weight the air could carry. It seemed to press down on me as I walked along the street back to our house. Ma had breakfast ready and I was sure relieved to find it wasn't rice pudding. Instead there were the last of the strawberries from our garden and leftover mashed potatoes made into crispy cakes. Eating times had not changed with either our move into town or Pa's passing. We ate without talking. No one asked about how my paper route had gone or how the other boys were. While she was cleaning up, Ma did ask me about Wally's mother's wrist but since I didn't know that conversation didn't go anywhere. Once I had finished my chores, I found my book and slipped quietly away into the back shed. It was *Kidnapped*. I had just discovered Robert Louis Stevenson during my last year of school. He was now my favorite author. It would take me a long time though to read all his books. They weren't easy to read and he wrote a lot of them. But I was always glad to have time to read and I had more for it since we had moved to town. There were not nearly so many chores to be done as there had been on the farm. There were no eggs to gather or cows to feed. There were no pigs to corral and no fences to repair with Pa. By the time summer ended I had finished all of *Kidnapped* and had read two more of Mr. Stevenson's books. The dime novels I read in between didn't really count.

When the new school year started it was still as hot as ever. But after September the mercury dropped and by October the air already had started to have a winter chill. That's my birthday month - October. On the day of my birthday the sun came out. It was a school day so it began with the five oldest of us kids getting ready to walk to school. The five of us tumbled out the door checking and rechecking to make sure we had everything we needed. A chorus of "Do you have your lunch pail?" "Where's my pencil box?" and "Wait! I forgot my cap," accompanied us across the threshold. On that particular day, a ripe-peach sky greeted us as we made our way into the world. Off we marched, clustered together at the beginning but then breaking off into separate clumps. I led the way with my fast-paced walk that no one else could or wanted to copy. I really had no patience with their dawdling and hoped to catch up with my friends closer to school. That was unlikely though since like every other school day I would be the first to arrive. Closest behind me were Maude and Mabel who as always walked arm-in-arm. Honestly, I could not begin to guess what they could have to talk about every single school morning but whatever it was, it kept them busy right up to the school door. Chilly and Clayton were farther behind. They had to look in every single tree cavity, climb every single garden wall, kick every single rock, of a large enough size, and make every stick into a sword. I was always tempted just to let them wander off and never get to school but Ma would have skinned me alive so I yelled back at them periodically. "Come on! It's gonna take all day at the rate you're going."

One way or another we all arrived at the red brick building which was our school. We headed to our separate rooms, hung up our caps and jackets and put our lunch pails on the shelf. Miss Gwynne, my teacher that year, always gave me jobs to do since I was the first to arrive. I cleaned erasers, filled ink wells and straightened rows of desks. After our first greeting and the assigning of my chores, Miss Gwynne and I said no more to each other. Naturally she was busy preparing for the day and I was occupied with my chores. Soon the other early arrivals would begin to appear. Lucy Beckman was usually one of these. She and her four brothers lived almost next door to the school. It was a big stucco house with dark green shutters. The Beckmans were people with money. Mrs. Beckman was one of the women who brought her laundry to Ma.

Lucy didn't look my way or speak to me but went straight to her desk and sat down. Not really because she was rich and I wasn't. It was just one of those understood things. A few more trickled in after Lucy but I kept right on doing my chores, waiting for one of my friends to arrive. Finally, Wally Berg gave me a little push from behind. "Philly-boy," he whispered, "whadda 'ya doin? Teacher's pet?" I gave him a push back, harder, then Miss Gwynne looked up at both of us so we stopped. Wally's arrival was followed by a whole rush of other boys and girls. The school day was just about to begin so just about everybody was there. Ollie Stuckman was not there and would probably be late. He was usually late or not there at all. I never knew why. They had a hard time over at their place, Ma said, so maybe that was why. Ollie was the kind of kid who was easy to tease. His hair stuck every which way and his clothes had patches on the patches. He also wore bib-overalls like the country kids. Most of the town boys wore knickerbockers. Ollie was the littlest, skinniest kid in our grade and a few grades lower. And this was true even though he must have been at least two years older than the rest of us. I suppose he was one of the few kids in class whose family was poorer than ours.

Spider MacDonald sat in the desk right in front of me. The row was MacDonald, then McCoy, Ray Munson, and so on. Miss Gwynne called him John and I imagine so did his mother but everyone else called him Spider. He was long limbed, had dark, oily hair and wore glasses - a spider. He was, however, not one of those spiders that dart into dark places before you can put a jar over it and save it for later so you can put it on your sister's pillow. He was more the sleepy, creeping kind who might be great on the basketball team because he was so tall but turned out not to be because he was so slow. He even smelled like a crawly little animal. He was forever turning his hot, sour breath on me to ask me to show him how to do the arithmetic problem Miss Gwynne had just given us, or to stretch his long knobby finger on the page we were reading and ask me what "perspiration" meant.

"Sweat, now turn around and do your own reading."

"Sweat? Why don't he just say sweat if that's what it is?"

How do you answer a question like that? "Because he wanted a four-syllable word instead of a one-syllable word, I guess. Miss Gwynne is looking at us. Get back to work."

He turned in protest, "Nothing wrong with sweat."

To Spider, our lessons seemed like a chore that had no point, like an exclusive club he had not been given the secret handshake for. I felt sorry for him because as long as he was sitting in that classroom, in that desk, I could see he was miserable. As soon as the school day ended and we were outside his face broke into a toothy grin and he was ready for anything - especially anything that involved mischief. He was an expert at egging a house, for example, and could even manage to get up some speed when the house owner, who we thought was out, stepped onto his front porch. When we were older he would mastermind the relocation of an outhouse that would be one of our finest accomplishments. But, for Spider, school was a maze with no way out.

To me, on the other hand, it all made sense. The arithmetic, I could mostly do in my head. I liked the way it worked together like a puzzle. If I multiplied 8 by 7 and got 56, then I could divide 56 by 7 and get 8. Numbers seemed to have a sort of magic. They were real and made-up at the same time.

Reading though was my best subject. When I read a book, I could be anybody and I could go anywhere. Like *Treasure Island* - that was a story any boy could imagine himself in. There I was on a schooner, out on the open sea, bound for treasure - and adventure. Though only a young lad I was wily and brave. I could hold my own with those buccaneers. Hidden out of sight I would overhear their plans and devise a plan of my own. I would...

"Philip! Put that book down and take out your arithmetic!" I was certainly lucky it was Miss Gwynne. Most of the other teachers would have had me hold my hand out while they slapped it with a ruler. Boy did that smart. Miss Mies, who had been my teacher the year before, never let a day go by without thwhacking someone with her ruler. We generally called her Miss Mice behind her back. She had a pointy, little nose and grayish hair. The only problem was remembering when you were behind her back and when you were not.

"Philip McCoy, did you just hand a piece of candy under your desk to John MacDonald?"

"No, Miss Mice." Thwack!

Miss Gwynne preferred shaming to the ruler. "Philip, come up to the front of the class and write your division problems on the board." Everyone giggled. Partly they giggled because I was going to look silly standing with my back to the class writing on the blackboard which was twice as high as me, hoping my answers were right, but partly they giggled because they were nervous that Miss Gwynne would catch them at something and call them up front of the class. You can just imagine how much Spider MacDonald liked being in front of the class, doing his arithmetic on the board. Secretly, I didn't really mind so much writing my work on the board. I was pretty sure I had the answer right and besides I liked getting the chance to hold that fat, round piece of chalk. I liked the way it made the numbers stand up straight and how it made a fine dust in my hands. Of course, I made sure it seemed like I hated being there. Otherwise the rest of the class would be disappointed and, worse, Miss Gwynne would have to come up with another way to mortify me.

"Time for recess class."

On the way out the door, for no particular reason, Carl Christensen pushed Ollie Stuckman on the ground hard. Maybe he had gotten in Carl's way in the stampede out of the building. I don't know. Ollie got pushed on the ground pretty regularly. When I told Ma about it later, which was a mistake, she said, "Now, don't you let that Christensen boy pick on little Ollie. That ain't right."

"But Ma," I said, "what can I do about it?"

"You can tell the teacher. That's what."

Ma, of course, lived in that foreign country called adulthood and did not at all understand the rituals and customs of the world I lived in. Tell on Carl Christensen to the teacher? Sure, and I could walk straight into a burning building too. I never told the teacher anything but I did stand around close to Ollie during the rest of recess. Carl left him alone and went and picked on some other skinny kid, but Ollie was bound to have his turn again some time. There was nothing in the world I could do about that. One day Ollie though would turn on Carl. He would take his revenge with a fury. But that day was still in the future.

Recess was almost everybody's favorite part of the school day. It was certainly Spider's. I guess I liked the chance for a break. I am pretty sure Ollie Stuckman hated it.

The first thing we boys did was get ready for a game of red rover. Who started it? Hard to say but we didn't have long so we scrambled to divide into an east side and a west side. I grabbed Ollie Stuckman's hand and Al Scobie took my other. Al looked across me at Ollie with a funny expression. Ollie didn't usually play games at recess. Al didn't object though. He was pretty fair-minded.

"Red rover, red rover send Jim right over." This was a good start. Jim Dodd couldn't break through a paper bag. Head down, legs churning he did his best to force our hands apart but instead we had another 'man' on our side. "Red rover, red rover send Spider right over." I wish you could see Spider run. His arms move as much as his legs do. They are long and gangly and whirl around in big circles as if they were in slow motion. And, would you believe it? He broke through the line and brought Carl Christensen back with him. Like I said Spider was smarter outside than he was inside the school.

"Red rover, red rover, send".... I was afraid they were going to yell Ollie which would have made sense but could be a disaster. They didn't. Instead they yelled, "...Phil right over." I don't know what I look like when I run but I can run fast. I picked the weakest link I could see and ran as hard as I could.

Then I was on my back on the ground.

"What happened?" I heard myself say through a fog in my brain. Everyone around me was screaming and jumping up and down. Next to me I could see Wally Berg also lying flat on his back.

"What happened?"

"You ran into me."

"What were you doing in my way?" I wanted to take a swing at him but my head was swimming and I didn't feel so good.

"I guess I was talking to Al and I didn't see you comin'"

Above me I could see teachers standing over us. They were, of course, going to ask a lot of questions and try to sort the whole thing out. Worse still the game of red rover was over and so would recess soon be. Someone in the crowd handed me a warm, wet rag which was the first time I realized my nose was bleeding. One of the teachers reached down to help me up, brushed me off and asked me if I could walk back into the schoolhouse on my own.

"Sure." I said even though I wasn't too sure. I was hoping nobody would notice how wobbly my legs were so I walked really slow and kept that blood-soaked rag balled up against my nose. Then I felt someone put his arm under mine. It was Ollie Stuckman. People can sure be surprising.

Miss Coot, the school nurse, made me lie down on a cot after recess was over. I must have been worse off than Wally Berg because he was nowhere in sight. My nose had stopped bleeding but my head was throbbing like something was knocking around inside. Next to me on the floor was a bucket. Miss Coot must have put it there just in case. On the whole, it was adding up to be a pretty discouraging birthday.

I spent the rest of the afternoon on the cot. I didn't want to but I couldn't seem to stand up without the room see-sawing. After a while Miss Gwynne came in and told me not to worry. The class was reviewing things I already knew. I must have fallen asleep when she left because the next thing I knew the school bell rang. For a minute I couldn't figure out where I was or remember what had happened. Then my head exploded - at least it felt like that. I made myself get up though. I couldn't stand to be on that cot any more. Miss Coot had gone so there was no one to stop me.

When I got out to the hall, it was empty. Teachers were probably still in their rooms but there wasn't a student in sight. Outside clouds were now covering what had been a warming sun. There was even a cold breeze and I had a slow, miserable walk home. My birthday couldn't get much worse unless we had rice pudding for supper.

"What happened to you!" Ma gasped when she saw me.

I looked in the mirror above the dresser. On my forehead was a lump the size of a chicken egg. The left side of my face had a long scrape and was embedded with bits of pea gravel. Under my nose was a smear of dried blood.

"I'll get you a bath ready."

A bath on a Tuesday? Ma must have lost her marbles.

"I don't need a bath." I weakly protested. A bath sounded wonderful.

"Plenty hot," I added.

I soaked in that water until I had raisin fingers. No one else got in the water after me - not even Ma.

Ma put out a clean shirt for me. I had two shirts. The one I had been wearing was bloody and dirty.

All of me felt better after my bath. Even my head throbbed less. But I was confused about all the fuss Ma was making. I followed her around and told her all about the game of red rover. That's when she told me to tell the teacher about Carl pushing Ollie Stuckman on the ground. She was only half listening though I could tell so finally I left her alone and went outside to find my brothers.

"Did someone beat you up?" Chilly asked.

"No. What are you doin'?"

"Makin' a pile of leaves to jump into," he stopped for a second, "like we used to with Pa."

Our Uncle Ted pulled up while we were making our pretty average pile of leaves.

"You folks ready to go?" He said with a big grin. Then he added, "I hope the other guy looks worse than you."

I just said, "Go?"

"Didn't your ma tell you we're having a party?"

A party? Our family didn't have parties. It turned out though that there was going to be a birthday party for me at my aunt and uncle's house. In my whole life no one had ever thrown a party for me. I could hardly believe it. When me and Ma and my brothers and sisters arrived, everyone was there - my cousins, aunts, uncles, grandparents. There were colored streamers and balloons. Two tables had been set for supper. The bigger table was for the grownups. Right next to it was a smaller table for the kids. Next to each place at the kids table, there was a three-cornered cap like the kind the Three Musketeers wore. Someone had folded newspapers into hats and stuck a colored feather in the back of each.

I grabbed the cap that was at the head of the table which I guessed was my place, put it on my head, turned to my sister Maude and crossed my eyes. She put a cap on her head and stuck out her tongue. This was going to be a great party.

There was general chaos as everyone talked at once - greeting each other and asking me by turn, "Did you walk into a wall?" or "Did Chilly finally take a swing at you?" No one wanted an answer of course. They just wanted to say something silly and then laugh at how funny they were. Finally, Aunt Maude said we had to sit down or the food was going to get cold. Each table was crowded with plates and bowls and platters filled with food of every kind. It seemed like all my favorites were there - mashed potatoes and gravy, biscuits and honey, slices of roast beef, applesauce and watermelon pickles.

My aunt and uncle weren't all that much better off than we were. They had a pa at their house though and that made a lot of difference. But I think maybe everyone just felt like having a party. It had been a hard year in our family.

After we had devoured the main course, Aunt Maude disappeared into the kitchen and came back carrying a cake on stand. It had a lit candle stuck in the middle. She put it down right in front of me. The kids yelled together, "Make a wish! Make a wish!" I closed my eyes but I couldn't think of anything to wish for that could actually come true so I just waited a second, opened my eyes and blew out the candle. Aunt Ellie started everyone on "Happy Birthday to You." Next to me I could hear my cousin Cecil singing in a whisper, "Happy Birthday to you! You belong in a zoo. You look like a monkey and smell like one too." I reached under the table and grabbed some flesh from his arm and squeezed it as hard as I could.

It was Grandma's banana cake. Oh boy. After I wolfed down my slice, I opened my stack of birthday cards. They were all handmade by my sisters, brothers and cousins. One had a fish on the front which was really a circle with a triangle at the end. My little brother Bunny made that. He used a purple crayon. I had never seen a purple fish but I supposed there must be one. My cousin Daisy's card had so much glue on it that the front and back stuck together. The best one was Mabel's. On the front of hers, she had made a crescent moon with glitter. It made me think of fall nights when we lived on the farm. There was no card with it but next to the stack was a little package about three inches long. I tore off the wrapper. Inside was a pocket knife. My own pocket knife. Pa had always said I should have one. It wasn't brand new or anything but it had been polished until it almost gleamed. It was a beauty. I looked up and Ma smiled so I knew it was from her. I couldn't really say anything - not without crying - so I just smiled back. Just then Uncle Ted cleared his throat really loudly like he didn't really need to clear his throat but more like he just wanted to say something. He was sitting at the head of the grownups table and everyone there and all the kids turned to look at him.

"Well now," he said as he looked around the room making sure he had everyone's attention, "I wonder what the poor people are doing tonight?"

None of us knew.

Chapter Eight: At Bat

I suppose if I had to make a chart like the kind the teacher sometimes puts on the blackboard it might have two columns. One side would list good things and the other column the bad things. At the top of the bad list would be Pa getting sick and dying. Our house catching on fire would be right up there too. Also my getting run into during a game of red rover. And, of course, rice pudding. The good column would have Uncle Vernon's visit, reading *Kidnapped*, and my surprise birthday party. It would also have sports. I like any kind of sport that I can think of. Football is maybe my favorite. But in the summer, nothing tops baseball.

I started playing baseball, or something like it, when we still lived on the farm. No one that I can remember ever taught me to play. Catching, throwing, batting a ball are all so basic I guess I figured them out by myself. When my pa was alive he never came out and threw the ball with me or my sisters or brothers. He had work to do. He did not really ever play any kind of game with us. But he was what you would call playful and he could make ordinary chores like getting the chicken in the gate into a kind of a game. Fishing with him was about my favorite thing in the world to do. My pa was an expert swimmer. On a hot summer day he would pile everyone but Ma and the baby into his truck and we would drive out to the lake and swim away most of the afternoon. But he never threw the ball with me.

Then there was Ma. It goes without saying that she never played baseball with me either. While she had a good heart I cannot say Ma was playful. My brothers were just too little to join in when I first started to play. They could not throw; they could not catch, and hitting was out of the question. Of course, they eventually got old enough to do these things but that was a long time coming in my opinion. That left my sisters. My best hope with them was bribery. It was not that they were not strong enough or coordinated enough. They were. They just weren't interested or, more accurately, they weren't as interested. I had to offer them an incentive. There were two good forms of incentive. One was candy and the other was chore-relief. Candy was by far the easiest. For one thing, I seemed to always have more candy than they did. That was not because I ate less candy, in fact, the opposite. But I got more candy. Why? There are many things in this life that are not fair and this is one of them. It was because I was a boy. Adults liked to give me candy. They patted my towheaded mop, smiled and handed me a piece of candy. I smiled back. Also, I had more opportunities to be around adults, and candy, for that matter, than my sisters. It was me Pa took with him on his dairy rounds. It was me that got to go into town to help him with his errands and it was me, therefore, who had earned a bag of candy. I had candy to spare, at least, for the right reason.

Chore-relief, being rarer, was an even better incentive than candy but it was a good deal more complicated. To begin with, I didn't even know how to do half the chores my sisters did. They might look easy but when it came right down to it there were mysteries involved that no boy my age was likely to solve. Food preparation was not so bad. In fact, if one of my sisters was not immediately at hand, Ma might have me shell the peas or even peel the potatoes. Beyond that though there was a world of spools and pins and knitting needles and balls of yarn that was clouded with such obscurity that a boy just had to shudder. In other words, chore-relief had to be selective. Even more difficult than that, however, is that it had to be secret. Adults were unable to grasp the real necessity and the true art of bribery. They seemed to take the view that it was a sort of pre-criminal activity. Therefore, it had to be hidden from them. Passing along a piece of candy or two did not set off any alarms although it might lead to surprise or even admiration. "Why Phil ain't that nice of you to share with Mabel?" It could almost make you feel guilty. Almost. Doing someone else's chores, however, could lead to dangerous suspicion. "Where is Maudie?

"I haven't seen her."

"Why are you mopping the floor when that's her job?" The tone here is rising irritation. There is no "ain't that nice of you."

When it came right down to it chore-relief could only be done when parents weren't around and when all your own chores were done. Swapping chores was not a form of bribery. I didn't really want to do my sisters' chores and they didn't want to do mine. The only way to get them outside to throw the ball, actually a wad of old rags, was to make a promise to perform some form of drudgery in the immediate future that they were required to do. Mopping the floor was a pretty good option because no one in the whole world likes to do it and there is no chance of breaking dishes or snarling up a ball of yarn. Not that I excelled at it. It seemed kind of pointless to me. Just as soon as you got it all clean, someone walked in and got it dirty again.

"You promised to mop the kitchen floor for me!" yelled Maudie as she punched me on the shoulder - hard. Her eyes were red and her nose was running so I guessed she was upset.

"I mopped it!" I give her a punch back but not so hard. She was still taller than me.

"What are you talking about?! There are big clumps of dirt pushed up in every corner of the kitchen floor. Ma is fit to be tied. It was my job so now I'm in big trouble." She had to stop and blow her nose.

"Where else was I supposed to put all the dirt?"

"Boys are so stupid!" She punched me again. This time really hard. "I am never, ever throwing the ball for you again. Ever!" She spun around and walked back to the house.

Never, ever was going to last at least a couple of days. I would have to turn to my older sister, Mabel. Mabel had recently been undergoing this disturbing transition into adulthood. She had, for example, started rolling her eyes at me when I suggested doing something completely ordinary like walking backwards from the backyard shed to the house.

I even offered to close my eyes while I did it - although that was really hard to do so I probably would have had to peek out just a little through my lashes. She didn't bother to say it was a dumb idea. She just rolled her eyes. She was rolling her eyes a lot lately. She also purposely talked to adults whenever she had the chance. Not just answering questions which we were supposed to do Ma said but actually getting into a whole big conversation with them about some boring topic. Like would the price of wheat fall again or would Marjorie Tower really marry Thorsten Kieker? I don't believe for a second that Mabel cared a bit about the price of wheat or Mr. Kieker - he was a biology teacher at the high school - but for some reason she suddenly had all kinds of opinions about both. She was not completely lost however as she still did pride herself on her powerful right arm. She could really get a pitch across the plate. Pretty accurate too. Some sunny days I could even talk her into a few pitches without any candy or chore-relief at all. But those days were rare and getting rarer.

After my painful encounter with Maudie, I approached Mabel carefully. She might have already heard that Ma was on the warpath.

"Do you wanna pitch a couple at me? C'mon."

She was in the house sitting by the kitchen window doing one of those things I told you about earlier. This one is where you have a bunch of yarn all wrapped up and then you unravel it and wrap it up again. Really! She was concentrating hard because it is usually a two-person job and she was doing it by herself. I was afraid she might ask me to help but I suppose she remembered the last time I helped and decided against it.

"Not now. I'm busy."

I waited for a while. Walked around the kitchen. Looked out where Ma was hanging up sheets. Then went back to her chair.

"Pretty please." Trying not to gag at my own bootlicking.

Even I could tell the yarn thing was not going well. She breathed out through her teeth in exasperation. "Okay, okay! What are you gonna do for me?"

I had really established a bad precedent.

"I dunno. What do you want me to do?" I was hoping hard that mops were not involved.

"Well, you could help me fix this mess I made!"

So I did. It took us the better part of an hour. She really had the thing tangled and I was not too good at my part. But in the end, we did it and still had some time to play ball. We ran out to the flattest part of the yard which was next to Ma's kitchen garden. We had to play parallel to that so I didn't accidentally hit a ball into the vegetables. Mae, that was Mabel's nickname, almost always pitched and I was batter.

She could hit the ball pretty good but she liked to pitch better and either was fine with me. We made a pitcher's mound by scraping up some dirt and used a piece of cardboard for home plate. A rag ball is more functional than you might think. You've got to have the rag strips pretty thin - but not too thin - and really, really tight. I couldn't make one myself. My hands were just too small and not strong enough. Can you believe that Ma made the one we were using? She did. Somehow the idea appealed to her and it was the kind of thing she was good at. It took her longer than I thought it would. Hours. She cut up the strips and pulled on them so tight. I think the major leaguers would have been happy to play with that ball.

Mae wound up. She knew to get her knee up and her foot way out in front. That's what made her pitches so fast. This one flew low across the plate and I yelled, "Ball one." Neither Mae or Maudie paid any attention to the count. I tried to explain to them how the game is played but I had to be careful because they might just give up and go back to the house if I talked too much.

"Let's just play," was their usual response.

An old mop handle was my bat. The best use for a mop as far as I could see. It wasn't like any old flimsy broom handle. It had been part of a mop used for scrubbing out a dairy barn. Long ago, somebody had given it to Pa when he

used to do his rounds picking up milk. Who knows why.
People had always given him things. Back when we had our
cow, Ma had put it in the shed and the cow had stepped on it.
What luck! Pa had let me borrow the rasp so I could smooth
off the broken end. It made a pretty good bat.

The next pitch was good but I didn't have my eye on it.
"Strike one!" Since I was the catcher too I had to run after
the ball as soon as it flew over the plate. I did this as fast as I
could so Mae did not have time to think. If she did, she might
decide it was time to go help get supper on the table. The
next one was just outside to my right. I reached out and whap
- contact. The ball would have gone inside the first base line
if there had been a first baseline so I ran. First base, second,
as fast as I could run - third and then home. I was so excited
I didn't notice that Mae had disappeared from the pitching
mound and had, no doubt, gone back in the house. For Pete's
sake. I couldn't wait for one of my brothers to get old enough
to play ball.

Opportunities to play baseball increased enormously
when our family moved into town. Our house was on the
north end of town and was close to St. Mary's which was a
school as well as a church. This was the church I had gone to
when I lived with the Bertrands and where the priest spoke
Latin which I didn't understand until later when I had to
conjugate a whole bunch of Latin verbs like amo which

means I love. I can actually conjugate the whole thing but you probably aren't that interested. Anyway, we lived near that church. Almost everyone at that end of town went to St. Mary's school instead of the regular school like I did.

There was a field by St. Mary's school where boys went to toss the ball around and I liked to go there and play with them. One spring day we were throwing the ball to each other and Wally Berg said, not to me, he just said it, "Man that Philly-boy has got a good arm."

I did have a pretty good arm and I could bat pretty good too. So they asked me to be on the team they were forming to play that summer. Nine Catholics and me. You probably remember how I learned some good German swear words back when I was at the Bertrands' place. Oma, the grandmother there, would let out a whole string of them whenever she was vexed which she was quite often - mostly with her daughter-in-law. She could swear a blue streak when she was in the mood. "Verdammt alles" was a favorite expression of hers but she would also whisper "Geh zum Teufel" behind Mrs. Bertrand's back. She, Mrs Bertrand, was so strict about rejecting the language of the old country that she did not know that Oma had just told her to go to the devil. I hate to think what would have happened if she did know. She could be very touchy when it came to Oma.

Wally Berg and the rest of the boys couldn't get enough of my yelling, "Geh zum Teufel" at one of the players from Lindstrom. They thought it was hilarious.

"Bull Larsson wouldn't know his rear end from a hole in the ground," Wally said. He said rear end because Mr. Havemeier was standing at the fence watching us play. It wasn't the regular season so he was the only adult around. He liked to hang around and watch us play. Sometimes he would call out suggestions like, "Tuck your right arm in and get the palm of your hand up!" But mostly he just watched. Bull Larsson was Lindstrom's third baseman which he was okay at but really not that good. But oh man could he hit the ball. He had just hit a long drive to left field and was running across home plate. He kept running even after he crossed the plate. I think it was hard for him to slow his bulk down. Anyway he ran right into me and knocked me to the ground. I wasn't hurt or anything but I yelled at him anyhow, "Geh zum Teufel." Wally and the other boys that heard that really cracked up. Bull Lindstrom started to give me a gesture but then glanced over at Mr. Havemeier so he stuck out his tongue. Stuck out his tongue! That really got everybody howling. And then Wally said the thing about his rear end.

Our first season was pretty good considering we were so new at playing together. While we didn't always beat the Lindstrom team we usually managed to make some good plays. We were learning and our coach, when we finally got one, made us talk over every play again and again. He said we needed more finesse. He said finesse like it rhymed with Chinese which is how I said it too until my teacher Miss Gwynne said it didn't. She said it was from the French which meant you never could guess how it was supposed to be pronounced. Anyway, the most exciting part of that season was not our new coach or one of our games against Lindstrom. It wasn't any of our games at all. And it didn't even happen until summer was over and the leaves were starting to turn.

So it was in the fall not the summer that Babe Ruth came to Sleepy Eye. He did. He really did. I'm not making it up. You can check and see. He was on a barnstorming tour with some other players. He and fellow Yankee Bob Meusel had been suspended for five weeks that season. Why? Because they went barnstorming. And what were they doing in our little town? They were barnstorming. Can you believe it? I guess they just wanted to play baseball more than anything.

There was a pretty big build up for that game. Everybody in town was talking about it. The newspapers all came and not just the local ones; there were reporters from the Cities too. I wished Pa had been there to see it. He would have loved all that hoopla. Ma was not too interested in the whole thing, "I don't know what all the fuss is about. It's just a game for heaven's sake." Honest. That's what she said when somebody asked her if she was going over to the ball field to watch the game. Just a game! Most of my friends went over with their pas. Al Scobie said I could go over with him and his pa but in the end my Uncle George came and got me and I went with him. Once we got over there to the ball field it didn't much matter who anyone had come with. Everybody was all smashed up against each other. I saw neighbors, people from across town, others from the farms, more from New Ulm and other towns around; some city people were there. What a crowd! The stands were filled to bursting and lots of people had to stand. We got there early - my uncle didn't want to miss any of the action - so we were lucky to be in the stands not too far above the home team dugout. We wedged in there tight but we had a great view of the field.

In my whole life I had never been any place so noisy. People talking, some shouting, many laughing, feet clomping against the stands, the band playing. All the sounds rose up together in a clattering din. I couldn't hardly make out what my uncle said - there was such a roar in my ears. At least I was so distracted by the racket I barely noticed how cold I was. For the middle of October it was chilly. Everybody in the crowd had on winter coats and wool hats. I could just about see my breath in the damp air. Once people had taken their seats and had pushed up against each other I started to warm up. Huddled together on the hard benches, we all waited in intense anticipation. Young and old, we made up a fellowship of baseball - united in our love of the game.

And then there he was - standing on the edge of the field. The crowd grew suddenly quiet when it spotted him. I guess he wasn't too imposing looking except we all knew what kind of player he was. He had hit thirty-five home runs that season alone. Someone had named him the Sultan of Swat and it was the perfect title. He was the king. Anything with a ball he could do. For a grownup his face was pretty pudgy. His fat cheeks made him look jolly which maybe he was. He had a big grin now and didn't look too worried about facing our local boys.

Each man in the line up came to bat and each at bat seemed to last a lifetime. Baseball is a game when at times nothing seems to happen at all. Your mind drifts like when you are in a boat with your pa or when the teacher is giving a lesson you already know. It's a pleasant sensation. You're not thinking or even thinking about thinking. You forget to think. But that pause in time only happened among us onlookers who were watching and waiting. On the field among the players there was no such lapse. All of them were in a state of acute readiness. Their muscles were tensed; bodies leaned forward; eyes were trained and pulses throbbed. When contact was made and the ball flew, the fans were the only ones suddenly alert. For the players, that moment was one part of a chain reaction - with each step set in motion by the ones before.

By the time the Babe finally came to bat, the restlessness of the crowd had started to get unfriendly. The fans were jittery and impatient. People shouted stupid things like the man two rows in front of us who stood up and called out, "Where did you learn how to swing that bat? From your grandmother?" He looked down at his friends for a reaction and they laughed but my uncle and others yelled at him to sit down and shut up. He did but not without looking around with a surly shake of his head. We had already lost interest in him though; we had turned back to the game.

And then the ball was gone. Before we could even remember how the pitcher had wound up and let it go - so fast it was a blur - the ball had flown away. We heard the crack later. After that we saw the arc. It took the ball so long to make its way up and over and beyond the field we had forgotten about the batter. When we looked back to find him, he was still standing to one side of home plate. He had not moved. Like us he had been watching the ball. Only when the ball had vanished beyond the stadium did he toss the bat to one side. Then instead of running the bases he headed back toward the dugout. Before he disappeared inside he turned with his happy grin and waved to the crowd. In response we poured out our adoration in one enormous howl. The next day, we read in the local paper that when he was questioned about his decision not to run the bases the Babe had said, "When you hit the ball that far you don't need to run."

There's no game quite like baseball.

Chapter Nine: A Spring Storm

Our second winter in town was like most in Minnesota - cold, snowy and long. Spring was always so slow in coming. But at last the weather started to warm. The snow melted into dingy piles mixed with dirt. The ice broke on the lake. First it came off in long chunks. Then the chunks got smaller and eventually disappeared. The level of the lake rose. While the ice and the snow melted, rain fell and it kept falling. The Cottonwood River rose two feet in one day. When the ice finished going out which took until the end of April, the river rose even more. The rain fell and it rose again. At the same time that it was rushing on to join the Minnesota River, the Cottonwood spilled up over its own banks. Bridges over the river creaked, stretched and twisted. In some places the span couldn't resist the force of the water any longer and broke. Heavy timbers flew up in the air like a boy playing with a giant set of Tinker Toys.

The town was full of news about the floods. Volunteers had been up all night building sandbag walls to try to limit the damage. No one had died but a couple of cows at the Bekke place had been swept away in the deluge. It was all very exciting. If the flooding wasn't enough of a thrill the wind had picked up in the night. Our neighbor, Mr. Gilles had stopped by before dawn to tell us that the highway was blocked by tree falls. That meant Boise Hopkins could not get through with the papers and even better than that school had been canceled for the day. We kids were free to roam. We could not wait to get outside and see what was going on. Ma was generally indifferent about our comings and goings. If we did our chores and were home for mealtimes, she was not too concerned about where we went and what we did. She didn't even ask us many questions when we got back home. As far as instructions went, the only thing she ever said was, "Behave yourselves." This admonition was so broad that we were forced to invent the particulars ourselves. It wasn't really all that hard to figure out. Permanent physical harm and extreme vandalism were out - though friends of mine and I would stretch the latter of these two on one future Halloween. The former was somewhat a question of degree. As far as social expectations went, we mostly took our cues from adults. If they cocked their heads to one side and smiled you were on the right track; if they knitted their brows and coughed into their fists, you had gone wrong somehow and you had better start over or get out of there - depending on how deep the knit and how loud the cough.

Today though Ma had decided it was best for us not to go out. Not go out? We couldn't believe it. On a day filled with such potential for adventure? She was convinced it would come to no good. It was pointless trying to reason with her once she had taken a stand. Maude and Mabel didn't even make the effort. They decided to ride out the storm inside. They would have fun with paper dolls and coloring. The coloring didn't sound too bad but I didn't get the attraction of cutting out little paper clothes and laying them out on top of little paper people. Maude and Mabel liked it though. The two youngest boys tried moping. I knew this would gain them no traction. For one thing, Ma didn't much notice if we were moping. She figured if we were being quiet we were better left alone. If she did happen to notice, she was irritated, "What have you got to mope around about? You've got everything a body needs - food, clothes, a place to sleep. Stop that sulking and leave me alone." And absolutely never, never tell Ma you don't have anything to do. I made that nearly fatal mistake more than once and always regretted it.

"If you ain't got nothing to do, go get the ladder out of the shed and bring it down to the cellar."

I got the ladder, brought it down to the cellar and set it up where she showed me next to a set of wooden shelves.

"Climb up as high as you can. That's good enough. Now hand me down them jars. Just one at a time!. I want to see why that shelve wiggles when I put things on it."

Then when I jerked my arm out and almost dropped one of the jars, "That little spider ain't gonna hurt you. It's more scared of you than you are of it. Hand me another jar and be careful."

Why do adults always say that? How do they know how scared a spider is? What do they have to be scared of anyways? If my ma didn't make me get a bunch of jars down I wouldn't ever go near its webby old lair. I certainly wouldn't crawl all over it and I never would dream of biting it. I was absolutely positive that I was more afraid of spiders than they were of me.

Instead of moping around or cutting out paper dolls, I grabbed a book and found a quiet place to read. At least if I wasn't going to have any adventures, I could read about them. Have you ever read *The Ransom of Red Chief*? You should if you haven't; it's hilarious. This boy gets kidnapped and drives his stupid captors crazy. I couldn't help but laugh out loud which was a mistake because all of a sudden my brother Chilly appeared.

"Go away."

"Whad ya' doin'?"

"Nothing, go away."

"Are ya readin' a story? Can you please read it to me. There's nothin' to do."

People can sure ruin things. Just about the last thing I wanted to do was read to my brother. He is not a bad kid. He's a couple years younger than me and I guess we look alike only I have blonder hair and he has these almond-shaped eyes. Our Aunt Ellie said his eyes were pretty which was ridiculous because he's a boy. But that didn't seem to stop her. She also said that they made him look like he might be Chinese which was also ridiculous. Mostly we're Irish. But that's how come he got his nickname. It's easy to get Willy out of Wilbur and then you mix that up with Chinese because of his eyes and you have Chilly. Silly but the name stuck.

"All right. I'll read to you but the story only has one picture and you have to sit still."

He sat down practically on top of me. I figured I had to start the story all over again which was okay because like I said it was funny. But it is a lot harder to read something out loud to someone than it is to read it to yourself. I had to go slow. We had only got through a couple of pages when I looked up to see Ma standing over us.

"I need you to go out." I couldn't believe my luck. But I tried not to look excited.

"I have Mrs. Olsen's laundry done and she's got to have it back today."

I was itching to get outside but I couldn't help but be puzzled. Mrs. Olsen had to have her laundry on a day when the wind was howling, trees were falling and the river was rising?

"They got her ma's funeral tomorrow." Oh right. You have to have clean laundry for a funeral.

"Can I go with?" Chilly didn't want to miss any of the fun.

I was relieved when Ma said, "No. I don't want to have to worry about the both of you out there."

I could see Chilly was crestfallen but I thought things were much better this way. I wasn't too eager to be responsible for him as well as the laundry. I stood up and followed Ma. She had the laundry all ready in a bundle and tied with a cord. On the outside of that she had wrapped a piece of waxed canvas. Mrs. Olsen probably didn't want wet linens and such for her ma's funeral.

"The wind has died down some but you've still got to be careful out there."

I grabbed the bundle - it was bulky and heavy - and went out before any of my other siblings spotted me. Once I was in the yard I looked around for our small, wooden wagon. I needed something to help carry that awkward bundle. The Olsens lived all the way across town. No telling what kind of trouble there would be if I dropped the thing. Even though the wind had died down some, it was still blowing pretty good. I found the wagon which was a trusted old thing we had brought from the farm. It came in handy for lots of uses. I sometimes carried the Sunday papers in it for delivery. On Sundays the papers are extra heavy. Ma had hauled a sack of seed potatoes in it last spring. She grew potatoes along the fence line and their yield lasted us most of the winter. She had also hauled a quarter beef in it all the way from the butcher shop. I don't remember her ever carting laundry in it. Mostly the people whose laundry it was dropped it off and picked it up. The women who came liked to stay and talk for awhile. Ma usually had coffee on so they might have a cup and chat about the weather and swap local gossip. I think Ma liked the company. Today Mrs. Olsen couldn't come and get her laundry though. She was busy getting ready to bury her ma.

The bottom of the wagon was full of old leaves and dirt churned up by the storm. I very carefully set the bundle down on the back stoop and cleaned the wagon out and then set the bundle down in it. I was just about to head out when I had the feeling someone was watching me. Have you ever had that feeling? It's funny that you know someone's there even though you can't see them. It was Chilly standing in the back doorway. He was watching me with that same disappointed expression on his face. I was sure lucky Ma had said he couldn't go or I might have been tempted to take him along just so I didn't have to feel guilty about leaving him behind.

"Stay there. Ma said you can't go," and then because I couldn't stand to see him like that I added, "I'll finish reading *The Ransom of Red Chief* as soon as I get back. Promise." I turned around and walked away without waiting to see if his expression had changed.

I went south along First Avenue. It sure was a mess. Trees were down everywhere. A page out of somebody's newspaper which had flown up and got caught against the Gilles's fence was still being held up by a steady wind. I pulled my jacket up around me and kept moving. Drops of water fell from the wind blown trees but the rain had stopped. Since I left our house I had not seen one other person outside. It was eerie in fact as the streets of our town

Page 186

are usually filled with people going some place or other. Or just out in their own yard. Right then the place seemed completely empty.

One lonely wagon passed me as I crossed Rice Street. I could see ahead that there was a downed power line on the other side of the street. A tree had fallen against one of the poles and had snapped it almost in half. The line lay slack on the ground. It didn't look like anything too dangerous but I knew not to go anywhere near it. Even the ground around could be electrified. I stayed on my side of the street and kept walking - faster now because the rain had just started up again. I hoped I could make it to Mrs. Olsen's without her linens getting wet. I knew Ma had trusted me with something that was important to her.

Whether it was because of the patter of the rain, or the wind that had never let up or even the scraping of the wagon wheels on the ground, I never heard the cry. The sound of it had flown up with the oak leaves which swirled around me in the air. I turned the corner at Elm and caught only a glimpse of someone suddenly hurrying in the other direction. Besides a man in the wagon, it was the first person I had seen since I left our house. I wasn't curious enough to turn around. He or maybe she was no doubt racing to get out of the rain. I was still dead set on getting to the Olsens' as fast as I could.

When I got there, I went around to the back of the house and knocked on the door. It was the middle of the day but the house was filled with people. That's the way it is when someone dies. When my pa died, we had a houseful for days. Ma's sisters and our grandmother cooked non-stop. Finally somebody heard me and came to the door. It was a lady I had never seen before. She didn't say anything; she just looked at me in a what-business-have-you-got-to-be-here way.

"I've got Mrs. Olsen's laundry. In the wagon. From my ma. It might get wet."

She looked behind me, "Oh! I see. Come on in."

I really didn't want to come on in. I wanted her to take the big bundle and let me go home. But I went back to the wagon, lifted up the wet bundle which seemed even heavier than when I left, and went inside while she held the door open. People in the kitchen turned around and looked at us but none of them was Mrs. Olsen. I guess she was sitting with her dead ma. It isn't respectful to leave dead people all alone until you put them in the ground. I knew a couple of adults in the kitchen and they nodded at me.

The lady said, "Let's put the laundry in the pantry shall we?" I followed her and did what she said and then I stood there. Ma forgot to tell me what to do about the money.

Page 188

Usually the women whose laundry it is pay her when they pick it up. I waited. The lady could see I was waiting.

"Would you like a cookie and a glass of milk?"

"No, thank you." I kept standing there but the lady must not have understood because she said, "Then you may as well be on your way." She talked like a teacher. She even looked like a teacher but not from my school.

"I think I'm supposed to get money or something." Something? Who knows why I said that. There was no something just the money that my family needed. I was ready to give up and let Ma sort it out later when the light finally dawned on the lady.

"Of course. Your mother needs to be paid for doing the laundry. Let me see what I can do."

She left and I went out and sat on the back step. That way I could see what the storm was doing and I could also get out of the middle of all those adults. In the distance I could hear the sound of a siren. It wasn't close by and it was growing fainter. The sound of a siren was not too regular in our town but with all the flooding and the wind it wasn't all that surprising. The lady finally came back. She handed me an envelope and said, "Millie says thank you." Millie is Mrs. Olsen's first name.

I got my wagon and started for home. At the beginning, I wasn't in a hurry so I went a different way. I didn't pass the intersection at Rice and First. Even if I had there would have been nothing to see. I did see a lot more trees down. One had fallen on a car and another had crushed a small shed. I could almost understand why Ma hadn't wanted us to go out. Then all of a sudden the sky opened up again and down came a … downpour. I ran as fast as I could dragging the wagon behind me. I was going to be happy to make it home and go back to reading to my brother.

When I walked in the back door I was drenched. It would be dramatic to say I could tell there was something wrong as soon as I came in the house but I couldn't. There was no one around but with the rain slashing against the side of the house and wind flapping the shingles it wasn't quiet. A kettle of something that Ma must have been seeing to had been left on the stove. That did seem odd. Ma didn't normally leave something unfinished. And that there was no one at all in the kitchen in the middle of the day was not usual. They couldn't very well have gone out in the storm after Ma had said nobody should go out. Except me that is.

I was dripping wet so before I did anything else I had to put on dry clothes. Our house was small. The short walk from the back door to the dresser told me that there really was no one home. At this point an adult would have been alarmed, started to worry, thought the worst. I, on the other hand, was pretty pleased with myself for having the good luck to show up when I had the place to myself. Since we moved to town, I could not remember a time when I had been alone in our house. I couldn't decide what to do first. What I did do before I did anything else was clean up the water I had tracked in. Then I found my book and a comfy spot and I settled down to read again. What could be better in the whole wide world than being alone with a book in a storm?

I had read almost to the end when I heard someone knocking at the back door. It was my grandpa. Ma's pa. Have I told you about him yet? He was not a cheerful person. You could even say he was grumpy. He seemed to have no time for kids. He had had six of them himself so you'd have thought that he would have been used to them by now. You would be wrong.

"I come to fetch you." He didn't talk much either.

My jacket was soaked through so I grabbed an old sweater ma had knit me. I climbed up into the wagon and sat next to Grandpa. Now I was worried. I didn't dare ask any questions though. I was afraid he might just snap at me. We rode in silence out to his and my grandma's place. When we arrived, Grandpa saw to the horse and the wagon. He didn't ask me to help. I didn't offer either. I never did feel too handy with horses and wagons. Some day I wanted to have a motor car. Until then I was happy to walk most places.

The house was dark from the outside. My grandparents didn't have electricity yet because Grandpa didn't much trust new things. When I went in my grandma came right to me. She reached out and put her hand on my shoulder. She was not much taller than me and she always smelled like the cubeb cigarettes she smoked. She didn't smoke them in public though - only at home. The only place I had ever seen a woman smoke in public was through the window of a passing passenger train. I think in the Cities you could see a lot of women smoking but I hadn't gone there yet.

"We'll just have to wait 'til your ma comes home to see how he is. There's hope yet. I just know it."

This was as mysterious as it was ominous. I wished I knew where my sisters and brothers were. One of my sisters was sure to know what was going on. Why I didn't just ask my grandma who 'he' was I'm not sure. I guess I assumed it was an old person - at least a grownup person. They were forever hurting themselves or getting some bad disease.

"You come in now and have a bite to eat. It might be awhile."

Food in my family was the great comforter. There was almost nothing that couldn't be made better with a bite to eat. I was hungry. It had been a long time since breakfast. Grandma laid out a spread of bread, butter, cold bacon, coffee, applesauce and three glasses of buttermilk. Of course,

Grandpa joined us. We ate our meal silently while I wished more than ever that Ma or one of my siblings would show up.

The next couple of hours dragged. I didn't have any books to read and the weather outside was as stormy as ever. Grandpa didn't ask me to do any chores. I did help there with chores sometimes when we went to visit but either Ma or my grandma told me what to do. I tried to guess what he might want me to do but when I thought of something I got worried that it might not be what he wanted or that I wouldn't do it right so I left it alone.

In a small room off their parlor, my grandparents had a piano. It might surprise you but it was Grandpa who could play it. Pretty good too. I went in there and looked at the piano for a while and then I looked through the music books. I couldn't tell what any of it meant but they were kind of interesting to look at. Grandpa didn't use the books when he played. I think the music was in his head. It was Uncle George who used the books. He could play too. I guess he wasn't as good at it as Grandpa but I liked it best when he played because the songs were more lively. If there were a lot of us together, my aunts and uncles and cousins, we would sing along which was to me the best use of a piano.

Grandma stayed in the kitchen and didn't bother me. She thought I was thinking about whatever it was that she thought I already knew about. I could hear her working even from where I was - banging around pots and such. It made me feel bad and I was almost ready to go in and ask her if I could help when I heard Ma's voice. Finally. But I could tell she was alone, not with my brothers and sisters, and that made me feel more uneasy than I had felt since Grandpa had picked me up hours before.

I stood at the kitchen door listening while Ma filled Grandma in.

"He's going to be okay they think. The hand is burned bad. He'll have quite a scar."

"They gonna keep him there tonight?"

"They are. They want to watch him but they think he'll be okay." She finally saw me standing at the door or had just decided to acknowledge that I was there. She nodded was all. She looked awful tired.

"It's lucky he didn't die. The doctor said that if he hadn't been able to drop the line he'd be dead."

The image of a downed power line and the sound of a siren swept over me. Then Chilly standing by the back door. And my never looking back.

"Ma?" I said. I didn't want to ask because I didn't want to know but I had to know so I asked, "Is it Chilly?"

She looked at me puzzled, "Of course Chilly. You didn't know he followed you?"

I didn't answer but went back through the house and sat back down on the piano bench. I couldn't keep from seeing my brother walking along behind me in the storm and then stopping to investigate that thick cable that was beckoning to him from the ground. It would be just like every walk he ever took to school - not able to leave anything untouched. How come I had known he was watching me from the back door when I left that day but I hadn't known he was walking all that way behind me? The hot tears were bitter and self-incriminating.

Ma came and found me, "Come along now. That cryin' ain't gonna do no good. Grandpa'll take us home and you can help me get supper on before the rest get back."

There was nothing I could do except go with her. I wiped my face with the sleeve of my sweater and swallowed back the bad taste in my mouth. The ride home lasted forever. No one spoke. Ma seemed exhausted and Grandpa was his usual tight-lipped self. When we finally got to our house, I followed Ma into the dark kitchen. Once she had hung her coat up and set her things down, she seemed to come alive again - opening and closing cupboards, telling me to go to the cellar for a can of stewed tomatoes. While she distracted herself with ordinary busy-ness, I moved around in a fog of foreboding. What would I do when the rest of the family came home? I didn't think I could stand the accusing looks I felt like I probably deserved.

It was just before supper time when our Aunt Ellie's husband Warren dropped off my sister and brothers. Nobody explained why they had gone to their house while I had gone to our grandparents but Mabel was the first to speak, "How is Wilbur, Ma? Is he home?"

"No, he's spending the night in the hospital. They think he'll be alright. They just want to watch him."

I couldn't bring myself to look at either of my sisters. My cheeks burned thinking they were sure to blame me for what had happened to Chilly. Who wouldn't? Neither of them said anything though and my two little brothers didn't seem to remember that anything was even wrong. They charged around the house with so much pent up energy that Ma scolded them, "Settle down. Clayton! Vernon! Stop that wrestling." Ma was not much of a yeller. I could tell she was on edge. Normally she would have told me to do something with the younger boys but she didn't this time. Maybe I couldn't be trust anymore.

We had a late, silent supper and went right to bed. Our house had one bedroom with two beds. One bed was for Ma and my sisters - the other was for us boys. Since my brother Bunny had moved to our bed from his crib, I had started sleeping on the floor. Three boys in a bed were enough. I lay down on my blankets but couldn't sleep - instead I listened to the wind and the rain. I was glad for the sound because it kept me from thinking too hard. It might hurt to think. I remembered that from when Pa died how much thinking could hurt.

In the morning, the world was still again. Uncle George came early to get Ma and take her to the hospital. I went out to deliver my papers. It felt so good to have a normal thing to do. It was a Saturday and everyone in town was outside cleaning up after the storm. That gave me a good idea. I got through my papers as fast as I could and rushed home. The girls were doing their chores. I still didn't feel quite ordinary around them but I could tell that little boys were in their way. That made my idea even better.

"You boys want to help me with something?" They looked at me with surprise. Ma wasn't even there to tell me I had to do something with them.

"Sure!" They both said it at the same time. We bundled up. The morning air was still cold.

"We're going to clean up the mess in the yard." I had my first doubts. Bunny had just turned three. "We need to pick up all the sticks and old dead leaves. We can put them in stacks and piles. Let's see who can pick up the most." That did it. Big smiles. We worked hard but had a good time. Clayton got the rhythm of it right away. He was pretty strong for a five year old. He made neat stacks of the larger of the small branches. Even though I don't think he meant to, he was leaving just the right-sized branches for Bunny to handle. I got out the rake and worked around the vegetable garden and along the fence line. Every few minutes Bunny would run over to me and proudly show me the branch he had picked up. His stack was pretty small so whenever he went in the opposite direction, and Clayton wasn't looking, I threw a small branch on his. The place was starting to look half-way tidy again. I was trying to decide what a good prize for the winner would be when Uncle George and Ma pulled up.

The boys and I brushed off dirt and leaves from our clothes and went in the house. Uncle George was carrying Chilly. George was Ma's brother and he had one of those thick handlebar mustaches that curled at each end. Because he was one of the kindest adults I knew the sight of my brother in his arms brought a thick lump to my throat. Also Chilly really didn't look strong enough to stand on his own. He was a gray-green color that I remembered seeing once before. My friend, Carl Christensen's sister had had consumption and she had been that color. They sent her away to some place in Arizona where she had gotten better and then died. I was really sorry to see my little brother be that color. He was so pitiful. His hand had a giant bandage wrapped around it and he held it up close to his chest. It must have hurt a lot.

Ma said to us boys, "Wilbur is going to have the bed to himself for awhile." I'll make up places to sleep for the rest of you for the time being. And you need to leave him be. He's going to need to be quiet." She got him all settled in the bed and then went back to the kitchen to get coffee for Uncle George. Bunny and Clayton followed - probably hoping for a piece of hard candy that our uncle always carried in his pocket. Maude and Mabel hovered around Chilly for a while - tucking in the blanket and propping up the pillow. He smiled weakly. While they were doing that I pulled out a tin box I kept under the bed. The box was painted black and had a latch with a small lock. I kept the tiny key on a string on a nail in the back of the closet. I suppose my sisters knew it was there but as far as I knew they had never rifled around in my box. I had lots of treasures inside including an arrowhead I had found on one of my rambles, the harmonica Uncle Vernon had given me and the pocket knife I had gotten for my birthday. I also kept my copy of *The Ransom of Red Chief* in there. My teacher Miss Gwynne had given it to me for helping her in the classroom. It was a slim book, the story was not even a whole novel but on the cover was a picture of the red-headed boy in the story shooting an arrow. Usually seeing that picture made me chuckle but now it didn't seem all that funny. I held the book behind my back and stood at the end of the bed. Chilly was looking awful tired and my sisters had done about all they could to make him comfortable.

"You should get some rest," Mabel said as she brushed Chilly's hair back from his forehead. It was sort of stuck there.

"Let's go and leave him alone," she said to Maude and me. The two of them walked to the door.

"I'll be there in just a minute." She looked back at me like she was going to argue but then her face softened and she turned and walked out with Maude.

I pulled the book from behind my back and gave it a last look. It had been the only book that I had ever owned.

I put the book on the bed next to Chilly. I didn't want to give it right to him because of his hurt hand.

"Here, this is for you. It's yours. I can read it to you or you can read yourself but I'm giving it to you. It's yours now."

"Thanks Phil," he said so softly I could almost not hear. "Thanks a lot. I might have you read it to me later. Thanks."

I left him then and went down to the kitchen to join the rest of the family.

I still wanted to show Ma how me and the little boys had cleaned up the yard.

Epilogue: The Drugstore Entrance

My first year of high school I made the football team. Weeks before school had even started in the fall, the coach had watched me run, tackle and handle the ball. I was pretty good at all of these so he said I was on the team. That meant I had to buy a uniform. This might have been a problem for me but I had earned some money the summer before hauling ice. I rode in the delivery truck with Mr. Lafferty. The back was filled with blocks of ice for customers who didn't have electric refrigerators yet. There were not too many of these left in town. Out in the country there were more. Mr. Lafferty drove the truck. It was my job, when we got to each customer on our route, to jump out, slip on a pair of leather gloves and grab the big set of tongs. The ice blocks were buried in sawdust in the back of the truck. I would grab one block with the tongs and carry it up to the back door where I was usually met by the lady of the house who would show me the way to the icebox. The slot for the ice was most often on the top of the icebox so I'd have to heave the block up and into place. I went as fast as I could especially on the hottest days when we had to move quickly between customers. As soon as I slid back into my seat, Mr. Lafferty was off to the next stop. I made a lot better money delivering ice than I ever had on my paper route. Also I got a lot stronger lifting those thirty or more pound blocks. That didn't hurt when I did my tryout for the football team.

Once I had enough put aside for a football uniform I turned the rest of the money over to Ma. Things at our house had gotten harder. More and more women in town had their own washing machines and fewer preferred hand laundered linens. Not many brought their washing to Ma any more. She had always been able to stretch what little we had. But the bigger we grew the bigger our appetites were. It isn't easy to feed six growing youngsters. Ma did the best she could to keep the family together but one by one our home emptied out.

First my oldest sister Mabel left for normal school. That's where people learn to be teachers. Mae was smart and I figured she would make a good teacher but I was sorry to see her go. There had been six of us for as long as I could remember. Ma was proud of Mae I think though with Ma it could be hard to tell.

"Teaching is a good job. You'll make good money."

"I don't know Ma. It might not be too good right away and I've got to go to finish school first." Mable seemed to say this as much to herself as to Ma. It was a big step.

"Them unions will help. They're gonna make sure people get what they deserve."

"You're right, Ma. They'll make a difference I know."

Maude was the next to go. She wasn't interested in more school. Instead she headed to Rochester to look for a job. She was what people called a stylish dresser. I never knew much about that kind of thing but she always looked pretty to me. When she was all gussied up she looked a lot older than seventeen. I figured she wouldn't have any problem getting a job in Rochester. It was a real city filled with shops and restaurants and hotels. I hated to see her leave though.

I guessed that Ma would miss having the girls around - not just for the help - though that too. It might get lonely for her with just us boys. I had never thought of that before. A grownup being lonely. I suppose Ma had been lonely for a long time. I just had never thought of that. I did notice one day that she still wore her wedding ring even though Pa had been dead for what seemed like a long time.

Chilly announced that he was leaving at the end of the year of school. While I had been hauling ice, he had been working on a big farm south and west of us. Room and board had come with the job and that sure helped make things easier at home. He told Ma he liked the work pretty well. He was a really hard worker and he was strong. He said his hand didn't hurt anymore. There still was a long scar though that ran all the way across the palm. I guessed that scar probably did ache when the weather changed.

Clayton and Bunny were still too young to think about leaving home but it occurred to me that it might not be too long before they did. Mable and I were the only ones who really loved school. The rest were restless for other experiences. For the time at least, we four boys were still at home and I was on the high school football team. Our regular season had gone well that fall and we had made it into the district playoffs. We were playing Pipestone on Friday night. The following night was Halloween so it promised to be a great weekend.

At game time the stands were completely full. I couldn't remember a game that had attracted so many people. I knew my uncles and a couple of my aunts were somewhere in the crowd. Chilly and Clayton had walked over too. Ma had not made it to any of our games. I wondered if Pa would have come; I supposed he would. For me and the rest of the team the tension in the locker room was building just like it did before every game. I always got this fluttery feeling. It wasn't just in my stomach. My head, arms, legs - all of me - felt woozy. I hated the feeling but I knew somehow I couldn't play without it.

Coach did not put me in the game during the first quarter. I sat on the bench. I hadn't figured on getting to play unless we had a good lead and it was late in the game. He wanted his senior players to get most of the action. That made sense to me except that the senior who also played running back was Harold Michelson. Hash. I'm not sure how he got that nickname but nobody called him Harold, not even Coach Reicich. Hash was okay. He was bigger than me. Not as quick but solid. He'd been acting funny though since the last game against Springfield. It had been a tough match from the start. Everyone was trying hard and by the last quarter even the strongest players were exhausted. Coach hadn't used me much. I had spent most of the game on the bench so that meant Hash had been on the field for most of the game. It wouldn't be long before the end of high school football for him and he was anxious to be in there as much as he could.

There were only three minutes still on the clock and Hash had just been handed the ball by our quarterback Pete Halle when one of the Springfield tackles slammed him. Hash went down like a ton of bricks - flat on his back. The ball flew out of bounds. Coach ran out and bent over him. We all could see he was trying to get Hash to say how he was but he didn't seem to be getting anywhere. Then all of sudden Hash shook his head, maybe to say, I'm not giving up yet? The next thing we knew he was on his feet and the crowding was cheering - even the Springfield fans. We won that game but Hash had not really been himself since. I mostly saw him at practice but some at school too. Usually he was a pretty easy-going guy with a corny sense of humor but lately he had been ready to bite your head off if you barely sneezed at him. He didn't seem to be much in the mood to crack jokes and at practice Coach had to explain every play to him over and over before he got it. I'm not too sure he ever did get it. I think he just pretended he did so the coach would leave him alone.

Hash was really the only player who stood between me and time on the field. Like I said I wasn't as sturdy as Hash but I was a lot faster. The game against Pipestone was pretty routine the whole first quarter and well into the second. They scored first but then we got a touchdown and so on. Right before halftime Pete passed the ball to Hash and Hash caught it but then just stood there. No kidding. It was just like he didn't have a clue what he was supposed to do with the ball. Pipestone took no time in taking advantage of that and before we knew it they were ahead. During halftime, we all went into the locker room while the high school band marched around on the field. Coach didn't yell at Hash or anything. He usually yelled quite a lot but when he was really mad he got quiet. He was really quiet then. I felt sorry for Hash. He was crying but I don't think it was only because Coach was upset I think it was because he knew that was it. No more high school football for him. He wasn't really college material so it really was the end. I hoped I was college material. That's what I most wanted to do - play football - in college and maybe even after. Maybe coach after that. It was a long shot I suppose but I knew the game better than anyone - except Coach maybe and I loved it. I would graduate in 1929 and then who knows?

When halftime was over, Hash came back out with the rest of the team which I gave him a lot of credit for. He sat on the bench with a blanket wrapped around him until the end of the game. At first, when Coach sent me in I could feel a dark cloud that was Hash sitting on the bench staring into space but then I picked up the rhythm of the game and played the best I could.

We lost, 27-20, but I think Coach was happy enough with my performance to set me up for the following year.

Hash disappeared at the end of the game. I didn't try to find him. If it had been me, I would have wanted to be left alone.

The rest of us headed into town after our showers. Things were hopping on Main Street as much as things hopped in our small town. A bunch of us went into Kuske's Drug Store for malts. I found a place toward the end of the long counter and Al Scobie sat next to me. The stool to my left was empty and I figured one of my teammates might take it but then the drugstore door opened and Ellen Schmidt and two of her friends walked in. They were looking all over for a place to sit but the place was as crowded as usual on a Friday night. I got up and waved to Ellen to take my seat. One of the other girls, Alice Cummings I think it was, took the empty stool to my left. Al didn't have much choice but to give up his seat to old Francis Knoss who stood there looking at him until he got up. Al and I stood behind the girls while we waited for our malts. Ellen was one of the prettiest girls in our class. Her hair was sort of reddish which I some people called strawberry blonde. She was pretty though and she smiled a lot and was fun to be around. Al and I were kind of in the way of people coming and going but we kept standing next to the girls partly because there was no place else to go and partly because the girls were cute. At least Alice, if it was Alice, and Ellen were cute. Francis was different. Not unpretty really but I would never have said she was cute. For one thing I don't ever remember seeing her smile. Why she didn't I have no idea. She was smart as a whip and had straight As in school but she just never seemed very chipper. She was Ellen's best friend though - at least that's what it seemed like.

Al was trying to edge himself away from behind Francis's chair toward Alice but he wasn't having much luck. For one thing I was in his way and I wasn't moving. My malt still hadn't come and anyway I was busy flirting with Ellen. I think I was flirting at least. I never quite knew when talking became flirting but I was doing my best and Ellen kept smiling and laughing so guess I was doing okay. The whole thing was much easier when the girl was willing to give you a chance. Which Ellen did - give me a chance that is. We hung out a Kuske's until it closed. A stool had finally opened up next to Alice so Al was happy and Francis whispered something to Ellen and then left. I took her seat. The place started to empty out so no one made us feel like we had to give up our places at the counter.

"What are you doing for Halloween?" Ellen asked me. I hadn't really thought about it but that didn't seem very imaginative so instead I said, "I guess I'll take off my skin and walk around in my bones." I grinned and she laughed. She had a pretty great laugh.

"How about you?"

"Francis is having a costume party at her house...just girls." I think she added the 'just girls' part so I didn't feel bad that I wasn't invited.

"Francis? She doesn't seem like the party type."

"You don't really know her. She's the bee's knees. So funny - in a cheeky sort of way." Ellen had aspirations of being a flapper. She liked to work some flapper lingo into her conversation when she could. Her parents, of course, would never let her wear short skirts or get her hair bobbed so that was the closest she was going to get for the time being.

"I like Francis. I really do. She just always seems serious and maybe a little stuck up?"

"Francis? I think she's just ready to not live in a small town. She wants to do something big with her life."

Didn't we all. The conversation stopped there though because George Bailey, the soda jerk who had made our malts, told us it was time to close up shop. We all headed out the door and parted company in front of Kuske's.

"See ya' in the funny papers," I said to Ellen as she walked away arm-in-arm with Alice or whoever it was. Ellen looked back at me and smiled. She had a pretty great smile.

"What are we gonna do tomorrow night?" I asked Al.

"What do you mean?"

"It's Halloween. We've got to do something."

"I suppose we do. We could meet up and decide when it starts to get dark."

"Where?"

"The cemetery on the north end of town?"

Not too original but I couldn't think of any alternative, "See ya there."

There were five of us the next night. Two of us had flashlights even though the moon was up and fairly bright. Nobody was in costume and we weren't expecting to get any treats. We had all outgrown that. We were exclusively on the tricks end of things now. Besides me and Al there was Wally Berg, Spider MacDonald and Carl Christensen. Spider had dropped out before we had all moved up to high school. It just never quite made sense to him. He had gotten a good job up in Le Sueur at the canning factory. He was living in a room at his aunt and uncle's there but he came home when he could. He was as spidery as ever but he already had started to seem older than the rest of us. Carl Christensen was Al's idea. I don't know that I would have included him. Tonight, even in the semi-dark, you could see that his face was a mess - both eyes were ringed with black and blue, his nose was broken and raw and he had a long slash still healing on his left cheek.

I hadn't been there when it happened but Wally Berg had and he had described it to me. They were down by the river - fishing I think. Carl had started making remarks about Lucy Beckman. He did that. I don't know why. I guess he thought it would impress the rest of us. We had all known each other for most of our lives. We weren't easily impressed. For one thing we knew absolutely that Carl Christensen had never gotten to first base with any girl let alone Lucy Beckman. She was beautiful, wealthy, smart and way out of his league. The stuff he said isn't worth repeating. I'm sure he made the others laugh but only because they were embarrassed. They were so used to it that they hardly heard what he was saying. But not Ollie Stuckman. He was with them that day and he was listening.

Do you remember him? When we were in elementary school he had been puny, underfed and dirty. But since then his ma had remarried. Her new husband was a guy who worked at the railroad. My ma said he was a good steady worker and Nell Stuckman was lucky to land him. I think she must have been right because things improved immensely at the Stuckmans'. Ollie started wearing clean clothes to school and stopped looking so woebegone. He also had grown more than a foot which made him taller than Carl Christensen. I guess Ollie knew Lucy Beckman the way we all knew each other at school. I doubt he had any idea of getting romantic with her. I think he was just fed up with Carl Christensen. Wally said that Carl had just made another remark about Lucy

- something stupid like where she had a mole that only he could have seen. He had kind of a pin brain. Ollie let him have it. Wally said Carl didn't even have time to defend himself. Ollie was like a demon. It took Wally and two others to pull him off Carl. By the time they had, the damage was done. Carl's face had been pulverized. Blood was pouring out of his nose and ears and he had a deep gash on his cheek. Someone tried to hold him up but they still had to keep Ollie back. He was ready to clobber him all over again. Wally didn't know what would have happened next but a car pulled up on the road above them and they knew they had better get Carl out of there fast. Two of them had to hold Carl up while they made their way along the overgrown bank of the Cottonwood River. It was slow going. Carl was barely conscious and a deadweight between them. Ollie kept following them, slashing through the brush behind them. Finally Wally turned around and yelled, "Scram!" Even that didn't get rid of him though; he just lagged further behind. Maybe he just wanted to see how things turned out.

Carl's mother was hysterical. I guess he really did look bad. They made up some story about him falling down the bank. She hardly listened. It probably never occurred to her that another boy would want to beat her sweet little Carl into a pulp because he was making lewd comments about a perfectly nice girl. The doctor who had fixed Carl up was a woman. The first in our county - Dr. Simone Engstrom. I call that irony. She did a good job though because he still looked more or less like Carl and he was ready to join us on our Halloween adventures.

The five of us were getting cold standing there in the cemetery. A piercing wind had come up and we had no place to go for protection. And we weren't getting anywhere in coming up with great prank ideas either. Spider was trying to talk us into egging some houses but no one was getting too excited about that. We had no eggs and stealing enough would take some time. Soaping windows was another suggestion. Soap wouldn't be hard to come by but then I was thinking this was not a prank that was likely to impress Ellen Schmidt.

"How about turning street signs around?" Not nearly dramatic enough. All these ideas seemed juvenile to us. We had done them all and while the memory of each made us happy we wanted something bigger.

"We could knock over some outhouses," Carl-meat-face Christensen offered. We laughed out loud at memories of past exploits in this department. Since we couldn't think of anything else we started off in the direction of the Snodgrasses' - the closest place with an outhouse on the north end of town. They actually had indoor plumbing but apparently Mr. Snodgrass liked to go out there just so he could be by himself. There were eleven kids in that family. We moved as silently as five fifteen-year old boys can move. We stopped short of the fence around the Snodgrass property. We needed to make a plan. A lot of not very quiet whispering took place. We still weren't all that excited about the outlandishness of our prank. Pretty old-hat really. Spider whispered, really talked right out loud only with a sort of raspiness, "Somebody over in Blue Earth county managed to get a corncrib completely intact all the way up on top of a barn. Farmer came out the next morning, headed out to feed his pigs and couldn't find the crib. Gone. Nowhere to be seen until he looked off toward his barn. There it was. On top of the barn." He was laughing so hard by the end of his story he had trouble getting the last part out.

Brilliant. I think I was the one who actually put the plan into words, "Let's do it. Instead of knocking the damn thing over, we'll move it." We had started to pepper the talk among ourselves with the word damn ever since we had moved to high school. The damn teacher, the damn desk, the damn hallway. We took pride in our increasing sophistication.

Where could we move the damn outhouse? We had no idea how to get it up on a barn or up anywhere. We'd have to stick to moving it to the funniest possible place that was ground level and we would need a wagon even to do that. Our family didn't own one so I didn't have to make the offer.

Spider's pa had offered to transport some holiday party goers in theirs. I wondered if they were going to Francis's but since Spider didn't have any sisters probably not. Carl felt like he was on thin ice at home. Once his mother had gotten over the initial shock of seeing his mashed up face she had grown suspicious of the explanation. Even Carl Christensen wasn't low enough to tell on Ollie. That left Wally.

Unfortunately the Bergs lived on the south end. We started our stealthy journey across town but when we came to the first cross street we realized that there were people outside everywhere. Our furtive little parade was going to go completely unnoticed by hosts of little ghosts and goblins and their supervising parents. I have to admit we were a little disappointed and were looking forward to getting back to our clandestine mode as soon as we got to Bergs'. But no one was home when we got there. The house was empty and dark.

"Oh, yeah. I forgot. They went to the bonfire," said Wally. This news momentarily stopped us in our tracks. Every Halloween there was a big bonfire in the empty lot next to the Methodist Church. There would be cider-making, taffy-pulling and apple-bobbing. It was a good time. But we were on a mission and couldn't be sidetracked by such kiddie fun. And it was going to be a lot easier to "borrow" the wagon when no one was there. Mr. Berg had a whole shed full of tools. He had hammers, ropes, screwdrivers, saws, shovels, crowbars. Without thinking how we might use any of them, we grabbed one of each. Wally got Jack out of his stall and hooked him up to the wagon. Taking a horse and wagon back through town was not going to be inconspicuous but we had come to the canny - to us at least - conclusion that the more we acted like we had nothing to hide the more we could keep our plans hidden.

In the end, we decided against going back to Snodgrasses' where a horse and wagon no matter how normal seeming would be too cumbersome. Instead we swung out west of town beyond the lake where houses were set further apart and farmland began. By this time, we had forgotten about stealth all together and had started singing our school fight song at the top of our lungs, "Skinny Minneapolis! Fat St. Paul! Sleepy Eye, Sleepy Eye beats 'em all! When you're up, you're up! When you're down, you're down! When you're up against Sleepy Eye you're upside down!"

Without anyone putting it into words, we had been all on the lookout for the first place that had no lights and looked like no one was home. This took more time than we thought and our high spirits started to mingle with growing apprehension. The landscape rolled so that each rise blocked our view ahead briefly. There were audible sighs at each crest that revealed only homes with lit windows. Finally we took a turn down a narrow county road, we were far outside of town by this time, and bingo. The first house we came to was dark. There was no wagon or truck in sight. A dog was barking but the sound was muffled so we guessed it was at the next place over. We pulled the wagon and Jack off the road onto a field opposite of the house. We left the tools in the wagon while we checked out the situation. It turned out that the outhouse was closer to the backdoor than was ideal but it was getting too late to find an alternative. Our first strategy was to line up on either side and start rocking the structure back and forth. You'd be surprised how well this works when all you want to do is knock the thing over. This outhouse, however, was pretty solidly made. It didn't budge.

Spider observed, "I think we should have brought a crowbar for this one."

Wally rolled his eyes, "We did! And it's back in the wagon."

"Oh yeah. That's right."

"I'll get it," Carl said before anyone else could offer. I had noticed that Carl had been acting not quite like his usual self all night. He seemed to really want our approval which I suppose he had always wanted only now he was going after it in a somewhat more agreeable way. He ran back while the rest of us pushed and rocked and shook the outhouse.

"Whose place is this?" Al asked. Good question. None of us knew. I had been down the road with my pa when I was little and he was making his rounds hauling milk. I didn't remember stopping here.

"You know there could be some old grandma asleep in the house." No one could disagree. There could be. I hoped she was deaf.

Carl returned with the crowbar and the shovel. I'm not sure why he brought the shovel. I for one didn't want to start digging around the outhouse. We all got to work. First we tried to wedge the crowbar in but the thing was tight as a drum. Four of us got on one side and sort of pushed and lifted at the same time. Finally we made a crack big enough for Carl to force the crowbar in. The harder we worked the louder we talked and the more we laughed. If Grandma was in the house she would have to have been dead not to hear us. We needed something to enlarge the small opening we had started. We searched all over the place - yelling and chortling as we went. Wally went along the back of the barn and came back with an old rusted piece of metal that tapered at one end. It might work. Three of us pushed as hard as we could while Carl put all his weight on the crowbar and Wally shoved the rusty metal in. It finally gave. One side was loose. If we had wanted to knock it over, we would have almost been there but we couldn't let go of our more ambitious plan - not when we were making progress. We started working on the other side. Same routine but we didn't have another metal shim to help. We rocked and pushed again. The more we pushed the harder we cracked up. At one point Spider just slid down the side of the outhouse wall and onto the ground. He was laughing so hard he couldn't stand up.

"Get up you damn fool. We've almost got it," Wally could barely get it out. He was laughing almost as hard as Spider. It was contagious.

"We've got to calm down or we're never gonna do it," this was from Carl who had been doing most of the work and was now dripping with sweat in the cold October air. We couldn't let ourselves down. We did our best to get back under control and made one last all-or-nothing effort. By the time the other side gave, we were too worn out to laugh any more. We gave a weak shout of victory and Wally went to get Jack and the wagon. Because the thing was so solid, we did surprisingly little damage getting it in the wagon. It was heavy though. We wrapped the rope around it and eased it down as slowly as its weight would allow. It took all five of us, two on one end and three on the other, pulling on the ends of the rope to keep it from crashing against the bottom of the wagon's bed. It landed with a final crunch and we threw the ends of the rope back on top of it. We tossed in the rest of the tools and headed back to town.

Spider said suddenly, "I sure hope Grandma doesn't have to use the biffy tonight." This beautifully crass image brought back gales of laughter. The night air was reviving us and we were ready for the last phase of our grand scheme.

We stayed to the west of town until we got all the way to Main Street and then we had to take the plunge and head right through downtown. Downtown was really just one street. There were a few cross streets with shops and other small businesses but the hotel, bank, drugstore, hardware store and movie theater were all on Main Street. Our biggest fear at this point was that Halloween might have kept people out and about. But since it was almost five in the morning we should have been more worried about people being up for the following day. We had better wrap things up. That meant deciding where the best place for an outhouse foyer was. We had our hearts set on the bank but when we pulled up front we were reminded that on either side of the entry door was a column. Ionic. We had learned that in our history class. The outhouse wouldn't fit between the columns and having it sit in front of them would spoil the effect. Besides didn't banks have night watchmen or something? Wally signaled for Jack to keep walking. We walked for another block and then there it was - Kuske's Drugstore. We had just been there, all of us except Spider that is, the night before. It was ideal. Poetic almost. Whatever that meant.

We had not really calculated the problem of getting a small building out of the back of the wagon. It was pretty well wedged. Not only did we still have to get it out of the wagon and in front of the drugstore, we had to remove a good section of the back so that a person entering through the front of the outhouse would walk all the way through to the door of Kuske's. That was the real genius of our plan. Before we could do that though we had to solve the problem of removing it from the wagon without breaking it to pieces.

Cardboard would come in handy. There was plenty in the large bins in the alley. Some of it was wet and greasy but beggars can't be choosers. We shoved the largest piece up under the end of the outhouse and picked back up the ends of the rope. When we had it part way up we figured we could tip it on the point resting on the end of the wagon. A fulcrum. We had learned that in science class. The five of us pulled with all our might. Once we had it almost all the way up it started to skate along on its own. Down it was going carried along by its own bulk. If Carl hadn't caught it in time it would have gone right out of the wagon and onto its back. He was not going to let that happen. I had to admire his dedication. Once we had it out of the wagon, we laid a trail of cardboard to the door of the drugstore and rocked and slid the outhouse on one side and then the other. We got kind of picky at the end. The whole night would be wasted if we started cutting corners now. We wanted to get it just right. We had to wiggle it back and forth - just a little more each

time. By now, we were dog-tired and increasingly conscious
of the fact that the town was already waking up. But just a
few more wiggles and we'd have it. Once we were almost
there we got the saw out of the wagon and cut a door-size
opening in the back. This step turned out to be the only easy
one of the night. The wood was dry as bone and sawed easily.
It was the only time I really gave much thought to the owners
of the outhouse. They were going to be much better off with
a new one that was less combustible.

Once we had the backside opening we were ready to
rock it into its final resting place. We crammed it up as tightly
as we could. Not bad. There was probably only an inch or
two between the back of the outhouse and the entry to the
drugstore. Our efforts finally had come to an end and we
stepped back to survey the results. No one spoke. We just
stood there and admired our handiwork.

We had done it - made a new entrance to the drug
store. You might have thought we had fulfilled some heroic
deed. To us I guess we had. We had marked a passage on our
way to the adulthood that was unavoidably approaching.

What a sight it would be when the first person - maybe
Mr. Kuske himself - arrived on Monday morning. Perfection.
We felt a little deflated by the recognition that Spider would
not be in town that day. He'd be back at work canning peas.
We ignored the fact that none of us would be there. The rest

would be sitting in our first period classes. We also chose not to think about the people who would be coming by the spot on Sunday. Kuske's would be closed but the remarkable presence of the outhouse would not go unnoticed. None of it ruined our sense of accomplishment. It wasn't about Monday really. It was about now and the five of us together. Nothing could take away our sweet sense of triumph.

Wally was the first to decide to head home. He had to get Jack and the wagon back - with any luck before his dad looked out his bedroom window at the back of their house and saw no wagon. We all had to go our separate ways. It was time to say good-bye and let our great adventure come to an end.

"Don't take any wooden nickels," someone called back as we moved away into the first light of dawn.

9 781952 493225